CONTEMPORARY STAIRCASES

CONTEMPORARY STAIRCASES

CATHERINE SLESSOR

MITCHELL BEAZLEY

front cover *Sheppard Robson, Shelley House, London, 1998*

back cover *David Chipperfield, Joseph Store, Sloane Avenue, London, 1997*

title page *Foster & Partners, Carré d'Art Cultural Centre, Nîmes, 1993*

contents page *Heinz Bienefeld, Haus Hefendehl, Kierspe, 1992*

CONTEMPORARY STAIRCASES

Catherine Slessor

Copyright © Octopus Publishing Group Ltd 2000

First published in Great Britain in 2000 by Mitchell Beazley, an imprint of Octopus Publishing Group Ltd, 2–4 Heron Quays, Docklands, London E14 4JP

Executive Editor **Mark Fletcher**
Deputy Art Director **Vivienne Brar**
Project Editor **John Jervis**
Designer **Colin Goody**
Editors **Kirsty Seymour-Ure** and **Penny Warren**
Production **Jessame Emms**
Picture Research **Claire Gouldstone**
Proof Reader **Sue Harper**
Indexer **Caroline Wilding**

A CIP catalogue record for this book is available from the British Library

ISBN 1 84000 316 2

Set in Univers and AvantGarde
Produced by Toppan Printing Co., (HK) Ltd.
Printed and bound in China

CONTENTS

"Naturally any staircase is a sort of machine to climb up by or descend, but in the best Beaux Arts interpretation it is a display, it is a dance."

Berthold Lubetkin, *A Commentary on Western Architecture*, 1975

A HISTORY OF STAIRCASES

Throughout the history of building, stairs have played a crucial part in the creation of spatial and formal relationships. But, long before the stair evolved as an element in its own right, it embodied a resonant and powerful symbolic dimension. Steps and stairs are common in the iconography of a host of different cultures, embracing and expressing notions of ascension, gradation and communication between various vertical levels, notably between this world and the intangible realms of the spirit. In Islamic tradition, for example, Mohammed saw a ladder that he climbed to reach God, while in the Egyptian system of hieroglyphs, steps constitute a very particular sign that defines the act of ascending. The Egyptian deity Osiris was invoked as "he who stands at the top of the stairs" and many Egyptian tombs have yielded amulets in the shape of ladders.

Stepped podia, such as this one on the Maison Carrée, Nîmes, were used in classical antiquity to elevate buildings above the ground plane, and place them in the landscape.

Christian iconography has many allusions to stairs. Jacob's ladder climbed up into the cloud, and the form of early Assyrian ramped temples emulated the way Genesis described the Tower of Babel as a path to heaven: "Go to, let us build a city and a tower whose top may reach unto heaven." The three steps leading to the altar in medieval churches symbolized faith, love and hope, and many pilgrimage staircases were constructed so that pilgrims would strive, step by step, to shed worldly concerns and attain a worthy goal.

The linking of high places and divinity is a constant theme in many religions and actual physical ascent is a test of faith. Many Buddhist temples, for example, are constructed in the form of steps to heaven. At the temple of Tai Shan in Shantung, China, a sacred

above *Jacob's fantastic vision of a ladder rising to heaven. Evoking notions of divine power through physical ascension, steps and staircases are prevalent in the iconography of all major religions.*

8

stepped path was built up the side of a mountain, so that the staircase became part of the mountain landscape, a daunting "skyladder" terminating in a shrine at its summit.

Stretching along a crescent of the Ganges, the waterfront in the Hindu holy city of Varanasi, India, is dominated by long flights of stone steps known as ghats – literally landings – where thousands of pilgrims and residents come for their ritual ablutions. Each of the ghats occupies its own place in the religious geography of the city and each swarms with bathers, Brahmin priests offering worship and people practising meditation and yoga.

Stairways resemble bridges; they lead to other zones. They can lead upward, to "on high". Mythical conceptions imagine a zone of power – high, superior, even divine. This symbolism is evident in the vast pyramid temples of pre-Columbian dynasties in Central and South America. Great flights of stairs soared to the summit where priests performed rites of sacrifice before a statue of the god. In mythic terms, downward leads to the oppressed, the darkness of chthonic space. The famous mid-eighteenth-century prison engravings by Piranesi depict a despairing, nightmarish subterranean realm of stairs and bridges leading nowhere.

The history of the staircase reflects the history of human invention. One of the stair's earliest incarnations was the climbing pole, which is still used by some West African tribes.

It consists of a treetrunk forked at the top to stabilize the pole during ascent, with notches cut in it to form treads and risers. Conventional ladders with twin supports and rungs were used by Native American tribes in New Mexico and Colorado to gain access to the upper floors and roof terraces of adobe houses. A more permanent form of ladder can be seen in the hand- and foot-holes hacked into the defensive walls of Moroccan cities.

Gradually, ladders, poles and ramped treads evolved into the first archetypal stair – the fixed, straight-flight stair. It has been found in excavations of buildings in Egypt and Mesopotamia and remains in common use today. It is the simplest stair in terms of layout since it does not require complex structural support and can be relatively easily accommodated within buildings.

Throughout antiquity, public and religious buildings were elevated above the ground. Even the most modest temple in the classical world was raised on a crepidoma, or stepped podium, and the number and size of steps were invested with symbolic and religious significance. A more dynamic and literal use of stepped forms occurred in Greek open-air theatres, such as the amphitheatre built around 350BC at Epidaurus. With its regimented rows of steps, it embodies an architecture of elegance and logic. Judging from such buildings, the Greeks can be credited with establishing a proportional relationship between tread and riser, now formally codified in modern building regulations.

Like the Greeks, the Romans used stepped podia for buildings. Unlike those of the Greeks, however, Roman temples were designed for public access, with spaces provided

above *Bursting with stairs, steps and ramps all frantically spiralling heavenward, Bruegel's depiction of the Tower of Babel is a dire warning of human presumption in trying to reach divine regions.*

for a congregation. The Maison Carrée at Nîmes in France is typical of this arrangement, with a direct flight of steps leading to a portico on the principal elevation. Yet despite their extraordinary talent for civil engineering, the Romans contributed little to the advancement of the stair, other than to take advantage of the load-bearing economy of the arch, exemplified by the tiered form of the Colosseum in Rome. In the first century BC, Vitruvius's *De architectura*, the first known text on architecture, says little about stairs beyond drawing attention to a need for stairwell illumination.

Until medieval times, the straight-flight stair pre-dominated. The emergence and development of the helical, or spiral, staircase coincided only with the rise of the craft guilds in the Middle Ages. Technically more complex and built principally of stone, the helical stair placed a greater reliance on the skills of its builders. Its intricate geometry and quality of steps, vaulting and newel posts preoccupied craftsmen for centuries.

The main advantage of a spiral form was that it occupied less space than a straight flight. It was also useful for defensive purposes. In medieval fortresses, internal circulation was devised to give defenders the advantage. Routes through castles were designed to be devious and narrow, and precipitous spiral stairs could be barricaded easily. Compelled to ascend in single file, a force of attackers could thus be kept at bay.

Most helical stairs were embedded within the walls of medieval castles and were steep, dark and uninviting. But as military architecture evolved from the beginning of the thirteenth century onward, the stair's role as an impediment to the enemy's approach became less important. Late medieval staircases were gradually transformed from dismal shafts into light-filled, sculptural objects. To achieve this, the stair was revealed by removing much of the surrounding walls, signalling a new period of expression. Many helical stairs were contained in free-standing towers placed outside the building envelope. The great stair constructed for the French king Francis I in the château of Blois, which may have been designed by Leonardo da Vinci, is perhaps the most notable example of a grand helical stair with dissolved walls. The stair is unusual because it looks outward rather than inward, through an ornate tower punctuated by large openings.

Dissolving the walls was only the first stage in the exploration of spatial possibilities suggested by the helical stair. There followed experiments to transform the solid newel (the central post around which the steps wind) into a hollow shaft or frame, so that light could be introduced down the middle of a stair. The discovery of the stairwell prompted dramatic new ways of experiencing space, connecting vertical floors and enhancing a sense of continuous spiralling progression. It also lent itself to expressiveness and grandeur.

The perfecting of the grand helical staircase was one of the major achievements of the Renaissance. One of the most influential stairs was built by Bramante for Pope Julius II, in the tower next to the Belvedere court (begun *c.*1505) in the Vatican, Rome. A gently

above *Monumental ziggurat (built c. AD 1000) at Chichén Itzá in Mexico. Great flights of steps soar up to a temple, where human and animal sacrifices were carried out to appease vengeful deities.*

right *The absence of a newel or central post for this helical stair in Gaudí's Sagrada Familia, Barcelona, allows light to penetrate down through the stairwell. Such stairs have a long history, evolving from their narrow fortified origins into gracefully fluid structures.*

inclined ramp spirals round an open stairwell (a form that later inspired Giuseppe Momo's famous helical 1930s exit stair in the Vatican Museum). Renaissance architects particularly appreciated the open well. Praise for Palladio's elegant open-welled helix in the Venetian monastery of Santa Maria della Carità marked a change in attitude from the scorn heaped on the staircase a century earlier by the art critic and architect Alberti, who stated: "The fewer staircases that are in a house and the less room they take up, the more convenient they are esteem'd."

In France and Germany, the double helix was particularly popular. Two stairs of equal diameter spiralled upward about a common centre, but began 180 degrees apart. Its origins are obscure, but it is a traditional Islamic device used in ancient minarets. By far the most famous double-helix stair, also possibly designed by Leonardo da Vinci, is at the palace of Chambord near Blois. The spiralling helixes form the hub around which the castle revolves.

During the Renaissance, straight-flight and helical forms were gradually superseded by the dog-leg. This had also been used in antiquity – one example is the grand staircase to the royal apartments in the palace at Knossos, Crete (c.1720BC). Two parallel straight flights connected by an intermediate landing, the dog-leg was a useful way of articulating space. It meant that stairs could be used to create a controlled perspective as well as to form part of a processional sequence. The Scala d'Oro in the Doge's Palace in Venice (1550) made use of the dog-leg in this way. The dissolution of the intermediate wall between flights changed the character of the dog-leg, liberating its potential as a visually continuous route and as a spatial connector and it became the precursor of the great open-welled stair of the Baroque period.

above *The high degree of medieval craftsmanship is clearly apparent in this stair at Rouen Cathedral. Stone is transformed into lace through the skill of master masons.*

left *The open-welled helical stair with very shallow risers built for the Vatican Museum in Rome by Giuseppe Momo in the 1930s was inspired by Renaissance models.*

During the mid-sixteenth century in Italy, the staircase was finally recognized as a potent architectural device. Vasari describes stairs in the 1586 edition of his *Lives of the Artists* as "the arms and legs of the building's body". Renaissance architects revelled in the potential of the stair as a decorative element and chose to increase the size and the volume of its container. In his design for the Biblioteca Laurenziana in Florence, Michelangelo transformed the stair into a free-standing sculpture of a cascading main flight flanked by two secondary stairs. The smooth flow of steps and sensuously curved treads mimic falling water.

Increasingly, the staircase occupied a central role in great public buildings. The simple corridor box of the flight was articulated and expanded and its walls were decorated with painted scenes and ornament. Subsequently, arches, columns, vaults and mouldings were used to break up the passage into a series of spaces to be experienced or revealed in a particular sequence. Such spatial choreography used false perspective to magnify and exaggerate dramatic scale. The Scala Regia in the Vatican, designed by Bernini in 1661, is a long, tapering flight that acts as a processional stage-set for the passage of the Pope to the Sistine Chapel. Tapering the geometry of spaces or steps changes the sense of distance and enhances the vertical scale of adjacent buildings and sculpture. Bernini's false perspective is a masterly solution to the problem of trying to fit a new staircase into a wedge-shaped space. Effectively, he transformed it into an ingenious, tunnel-vaulted colonnade of diminishing size, powerfully dramatized by light.

The history of the great Baroque stair is a history of a coterie of remarkable architects and their patrons, in an age strongly influenced by the fantasies of theatre-set design. The richest examples were in Germany and Austria, for example in the episcopal palace in Würzburg, built between 1729 and 1744 by Balthasar Neumann. These staircases

were sumptuous art objects that spectacularly transcended the simple business of rising from one floor to the next. Surrounding walls were dissolved by large windows, recesses, mirrors, sculpture and illusionistic devices such as *trompe l'oeil* paintings. On the stairs, the formalities of reception and departure were played out. The precise location in which visiting dignitaries were received on the stair was a telling indicator of rank and social position.

As the Age of Enlightenment drew to a close, extravagant palaces lost much of their relevance. In France, the Baroque became a despised symbol of the excesses of the monarchy. Following the American and French revolutions, the new republics espoused democratic ideals and became interested in restrained, formal Classicism. The power of the state was now invested in civic institutions, rather than in absolute monarchs. The new palaces were public buildings – museums, universities, courthouses, opera houses and theatres. Straight flights of stairs became fashionable once again. They were appropriately monumental, yet without extravagance, emphasizing the eminence and power of the state. Their generous dimensions, no longer necessary for ceremonial occasions, were essential to accommodate crowds of ordinary citizens who flocked through the buildings. Stair capacity and safety gradually became as important as location and effect.

Charles Garnier's great staircase in the foyer of the Paris Opéra set a pattern for resolving new safety codes, while also introducing a radically different way of envisaging theatre foyers. Recognizing that theatre patrons enjoy the social perambulation of the foyer as much as the performance on stage, Garnier's staircase is the architectural as well as the spatial centre of the building. It evokes the spectacle of exquisitely dressed opera-goers promenading against a backdrop of Neo-Baroque splendour.

above *The cascading pilgrimage staircase built for the Baroque Portuguese church of Bom Jesus do Monte at Braga forms a theatrical stage in the landscape. Every Whitsun thousands of pilgrims ascend the stair following a Way of the Cross, in a literal and symbolic ascent towards the divine.*

above *Teeming with human activity, the ghats, or stepped landings, along the banks of the sacred river Ganges at Varanasi form a great stage for the Hindu rituals of life and death.*

As well as the democratization of the grand stair, the nineteenth century was notable for rapid technical advances in the use of cast iron, steel and glass. This made it possible to construct functional staircases simply and economically, particularly as prefabricated kits of parts, for instance as in Decimus Burton's famous Palm House in Kew, England. Such advances also allowed the transmission of light into huge public stairhalls, transforming and animating the space. It was no longer necessary to paint the sky; increasingly large atria could now be roofed by naturally illuminated glass domes. Michelangelo's original

15

conception of a skylit courtyard as the vestibule for the Biblioteca Laurenziana became an inspiring model for a great number of nineteenth- and twentieth-century buildings.

The importance of the staircase was part of the grandeur of imperial architecture of the eighteenth- and nineteenth-century European powers. These ideals persisted into the twentieth century, but they were allied to an increased paring down and refinement of detail. Modernist architects elevated the stair to a compositionally significant element, using it as a freely placed feature to liberate internal space or to articulate building exteriors. At the Werkbund Exhibition Factory in Cologne in 1914, Walter Gropius and Adolf Meyer designed two transparent, equal, and symmetrically disposed stair towers in an essentially classical plan and elevation. The solidity of the entrance elevation forms a total contrast to the airy swirl of the twin staircases in steel and glass. Stylistically, Modernist architects were fascinated by industrial and marine structures. Balustrades were copied from ships and the bare-boned simplicity of industrial access stairs often constituted as powerful an image as the ornate classicism of the late nineteenth century.

As architecture fragmented and polarized during the postwar era, the primacy of the stair remained a crucial constant. Contemporary architects still find the staircase a supreme test of ingenuity both in terms of form and structure and in its broader role in the articulation of space. In the new British Library's main entrance hall, for instance, Colin St John Wilson's grand promenading stairway, with its balustrade sensuously wrapped in soft leather, conveys both the utility and the poetics of spatial progression. Even the modest and neglected fire-escape stair can be transformed into visual poetry, as Richard Rogers proved with the headquarters for Lloyd's in the City of London: although internally the stair has lost the battle of technology to be replaced by moving escalators, the fire-escape stair pods are pulled clear of the main building volume to create a gleaming, rhythmic set of staircase towers that dance above the city.

From the macro- to the microcosmic scale, designers such as Eva Jiricna have also employed the potential of engineering and materials to make staircases that resemble intricate, sparkling pieces of sculpture. They are a perfect synthesis of function and delight that grace a succession of shops and houses. Ever inventive and ever resourceful, Jiricna has elevated the staircase to new heights of tectonic display.

Jiricna's precious staircase jewels are worlds away from the climbing poles of primitive ancestry, but they aptly demonstrate the great distance travelled by a simple architectural device. They also demonstrate that, despite predictions of its demise in favour of elevators and escalators, the stair seems destined to remain a pivotal element of building iconography, continually refined and redefined, deeply rooted in architectural imagination and, more profoundly, in human consciousness itself.

left *During the twentieth century architects have exploited the potential of new materials and technologies in staircase design to dramatic effect. This concrete stair, designed by Eero Saarinen in the early 1950s for the General Motors Technical Center near Detroit, is suspended from steel tensile wires.*

below *The spiral cast-iron staircase in the Palm House at Kew Gardens, designed by Decimus Burton in the 1840s and made from a prefabricated kit of parts, is a combination of function, economy and visual delight.*

17

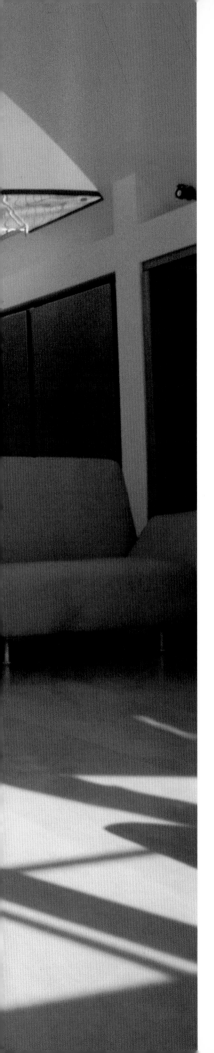

Far from being rendered obsolete by mechanical means of vertical circulation, the staircase continues to fascinate architects and designers. Whether straight or spiral, staircases are essentially structural elements, and their form reflects this inherent dynamic.

STRUCTURAL INVENTION

Abetted by the capabilities of materials such as steel and glass, many contemporary staircases are the epitome of structural ingenuity and refinement. Transformed into glittering pieces of sculpture as architects and engineers explore the potential of materials and structural systems, the staircase has gloriously transcended its primitive origins to become the compelling focus of internal space. Intricately constructed stairs weave and dart between floors, apparently floating in space, in virtuoso displays of strength and lightness, their engineering honed to the absolute minimum.

The combination of steel and glass has inspired designers to extraordinary heights of innovation. Steel is light yet very strong and can be contorted into fantastic, sinuous forms. Networks of tensile steel rods like gleaming lattices support staircases that seem poised effortlessly in space. The use of glass for treads and balustrades enhances a sense of ethereality and weightlessness. Light filters through the glass, generating a magical play of sparkling reflections. The work of designers such as Eva Jiricna, Richard Rogers and James Carpenter has advanced the development of staircase structures to new levels of breathtaking spectacle and invention.

Explicit articulation of structural elements in a stair for a loft conversion in Clerkenwell, London, by Alan Brookes.

One designer who has exploited the expressive structural potential of staircases is the American glass artist James Carpenter. Designer, sculptor, craftsman and consultant, Carpenter is at the same time an artist exploring new expressive possibilities and a technologist developing new types of glass and manufacturing techniques. Originally trained as an architect at the Rhode Island School of Design, Carpenter transferred to

JAMES CARPENTER
"TENSION NET" STAIRCASE, CHICAGO, 1996

sculpture, specializing in glass, and subsequently worked with Foster & Partners to develop a special photochemically etched glass for the Hong Kong & Shanghai Bank.

In 1996 Carpenter designed his "Tension Net" staircase, which connects two floors of a penthouse in a Chicago apartment block, forming a jewel-like set piece in the elegantly minimal interior. Since the thin floor slabs of the building could not support any additional loads, the staircase structure is suspended by steel tensile cables from the reinforced ceiling. Translucent glass treads cascade around a slender filigreed cone of stainless-steel mesh made of a double layer of steel rods, 3mm ($\frac{1}{8}$in) in diameter, spiralling in both directions. The mesh is stiffened by post-tensioning against the floor and by a series of compression rings set horizontally at 185mm (7¼in) intervals. It is further stiffened by the mass of the treads themselves. The cone was made off-site, with coupling points in each rod so that it could be dismantled into its three component parts for transportation. Once in place, the cone was stabilized vertically by means of a single turnbuckle thread at its base and tensioned by tightening ten bolts at the top. With its delicate spiralling rods, the structure resembles a vortex around which are spun the luminous glass panes of the treads and the slender steel balustrading.

Each tread is 30mm (1³⁄₁₆in) thick and is composed of three laminated layers of annealed glass, strengthened on two sides by nylon strips on aluminium bars; a composition that combines structural integrity and visual lightness. When damaged, laminated annealed glass is capable of temporarily sustaining loads and is therefore eminently suitable for such innovative explorations of structure and light. The surfaces of the treads are acid-etched, capturing the light and the shadowy patterns thrown both by people and by the structure itself. Carpenter's artistry finds remarkable expression in this dazzling, gravity-defying staircase sculpture.

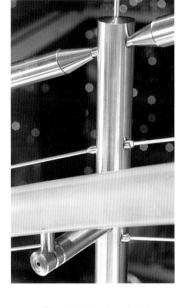

above The elegant, clean-lined wooden banister, artfully attached to stainless-steel poles, winds around the cone core of the staircase.

right A tribute to Carpenter's artistry and technological expertise, the staircase seems to hang unsupported from the ceiling.

above Glass treads snake around a cone of double-layered, stainless-steel rods, which is strengthened by a series of compression rings and tightened by post-tensioning.

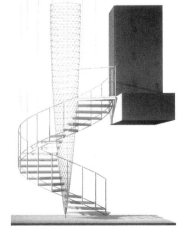

Elevation of the staircase

The Czech-born architect and interior designer Eva Jiricna has designed more than twenty staircases around the world, every one of which is a small masterpiece of engineering. Her great passion for certain materials, particularly metal and glass, is evident: "Using them is like learning a language," she says. "Each time you use them again you learn a new word." Jiricna collaborates closely with structural engineers to achieve the impossibly

EVA JIRICNA
JOSEPH STORE, LONDON, 1989

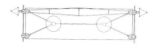

Plan of tread (above) and cross section through stair structure

transparent, disembodied effect she seeks. "For me a staircase is an opportunity for invention and escapism," she says. Her work is also proof that modern design methods can compete with the craftsmanship of the nineteenth century.

Key design details such as bolts, ties and struts of exquisite and calculated economy immediately identify a Jiricna stair assemblage. Typically, her stairs seem more like incredible pieces of sculpture than workaday interior elements. They are delicate, scintillating steel and glass lattices suspended in space.

Jiricna's practice is well versed in designing stairs for refined yet luxurious shops and has undertaken several commissions for Joseph Ettedgui in London, and nearly fifty for the Joan & David chain in the US. One of her earliest and most memorable commissions was for the Joseph store in London's Sloane Street in 1989. Jiricna has always been attracted by industrial materials, but in the Joseph staircase her architectural language of metal and glass reaches new heights of refinement. Replacing an existing spiral stair, a dramatic steel and glass staircase was slung between three floors, a single flight connecting each floor. (Jiricna considered keeping the spiral stair, but ultimately rejected the idea because of the obstruction to movement and sightlines that it created.)

To make room for the new stair, a hole was first punched through the middle of the three-storey store. To minimize the loss of trading space, the opening was designed to be as narrow as possible. Suspended from the second-floor slab and then laterally braced at each floor level, the staircase is an elaborate, sparkling cat's cradle of stainless-steel rods. Jiricna was careful to ensure that consistency of detail was employed throughout to establish a kit of parts that, when complete, creates a focus to which the various retail

above *Detail of the stringer which is made up of deceptively fragile-looking stainless-steel trusses. Each of these narrow rods has been prestressed to ensure its strength.*

left *Cascading through space, the glittering staircase is supported by an intricate lattice of stainless-steel rods. The stair provides a focal point on each floor.*

23

spaces on each level can relate in differing and dynamic ways. Enhanced by light shining through it both from above and below, the staircase is a triumph of architectural ingenuity.

The basic structure relies on trusses slung between four support rods. Each structural member has been meticulously reduced to its minimum possible thickness, so as to create a sense of weightlessness. The support system wraps around the stairway with rods progressively diminishing in circumference from top to bottom, reflecting the mooring

above *Detail of the glass treads. Each of these treads consists of a sandwich of clear float glass resting on an acrylic sheet. The sand-blasted longitudinal striations help to provide grip.*

point of the stair's suspended structure. Treads and landings are sandwiches of clear float glass 19mm (¾in) thick resting on 15mm (⅝in) thick acrylic sheet. Circular metal pads 180mm (7in) in diameter support each tread. The stringers are decoratively lacy steel trusses comprising 8mm (⁵⁄₁₆in) diameter steel rods prestressed for strength. Each glass tread is sand-blasted with longitudinal striations to provide a degree of grip. Balustrades are thin panels of clear toughened glass, and are held in place by steel trusses.

The stair's imaginative, formal complexity has both a visual and a structural justification, yet the structural engineering was entirely the outcome of intensive manual number-crunching rather than computer analysis, as might have been expected. Against a muted palette of internal finishes, its intricate structure and delicate transparency form a highly expressive contrast. The handling of materials and detailing is deliberately restrained, so that they act as a backdrop for the constructional bravura of the staircase. Walls, ceilings, screens and shelves, which are monolithically decorated in grey plaster, and creamy sandstone tiles on the floor all set off the stair to good effect. In certain areas, custom-designed slim glass shelves display clothes and accessories.

The elemental grandeur of the composition marks a peak in the careers of both Jiricna and her client and patron Joseph Ettedgui. Yet such is the transience of retail design that the stair no longer exists on site; it has since been removed and stored away. But this in fact emphasizes another aspect of the stair's design. Being entirely and meticulously prefabricated, it was dismantled and stored with ease when the time came to modify the interior. When it filled the space, it was a lyrical fusion of architecture and engineering and a powerful testament to Jiricna's extraordinary vision and skill. She is perhaps the ultimate contemporary staircase designer.

above *A muted palette of materials (creamy sandstone and grey plaster) acts as a calm, neutral backdrop to the sparkling set-piece staircase.*

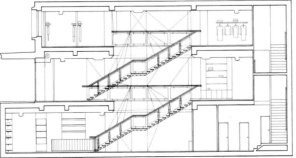

Long section through staircase

Luxurious materials, wide-open spaces, and exquisite detailing characterize this vast loft interior in New York's Soho area designed by Adam Yarinsky and Stephen Cassell of Architecture Research Office (ARO). But it is natural light that plays the most important role in the renovation of the duplex penthouse on the sixth and seventh floors of a former warehouse. The organization of the upper level was determined by the daily movement of

ARCHITECTURE RESEARCH OFFICE
LOFT CONVERSION, NEW YORK CITY, 1999

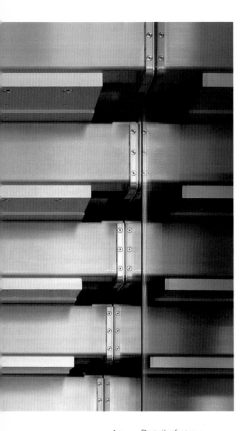

above *Detail of steps. Square tubular stainless-steel risers are fixed to aluminium subtreads.*

right *The staircase forms a powerful sculptural element in the New York loft's airy, open spaces. Although it appears to be a cantilevered structure, the risers are connected to each other by the aluminium subtreads, so that the load cascades down the steps and onto the floor.*

the sun and materials were selected for their ability to absorb, reflect and filter natural light.

The clients requested a classic loft that was as open as possible. The 650sq m (7000sq ft) residence is inserted into a pre-war warehouse that had long been stripped of its original interior structure. With a blank slate and an established relationship with the client (ARO renovated the lobby and designed new offices located downstairs), the architects have created new interior views and flowing spaces by opening up existing walls, floor and roof. A large skylight was added at the east end of the loft and the floor below it carved open, creating a double-height space that filters natural light into the master bedroom on the seventh floor. This atrium also brings sun down to the sixth floor, which houses bedrooms for the clients' children as well as an office and media room.

A smaller incision was made into the south-west portion of the roof, where an unusual staircase appears to float perilously between the open-plan dining and living room areas. Designed in collaboration with structural engineer Guy Nordenson, the stair is a prominent sculptural element on the main floor, providing access to a roof garden above, while defining discrete spaces within the open plan. Stainless-steel tube risers are supported at one end by a plane of laminated, tempered glass. The risers, which are connected by milled aluminium subtreads, are attached to the glass wall with milled aluminium U-brackets and wedges made from Delrin, a tough, versatile engineering plastic.

Large laminated glass panels provide the stair's impressive structural stability. The structure has two

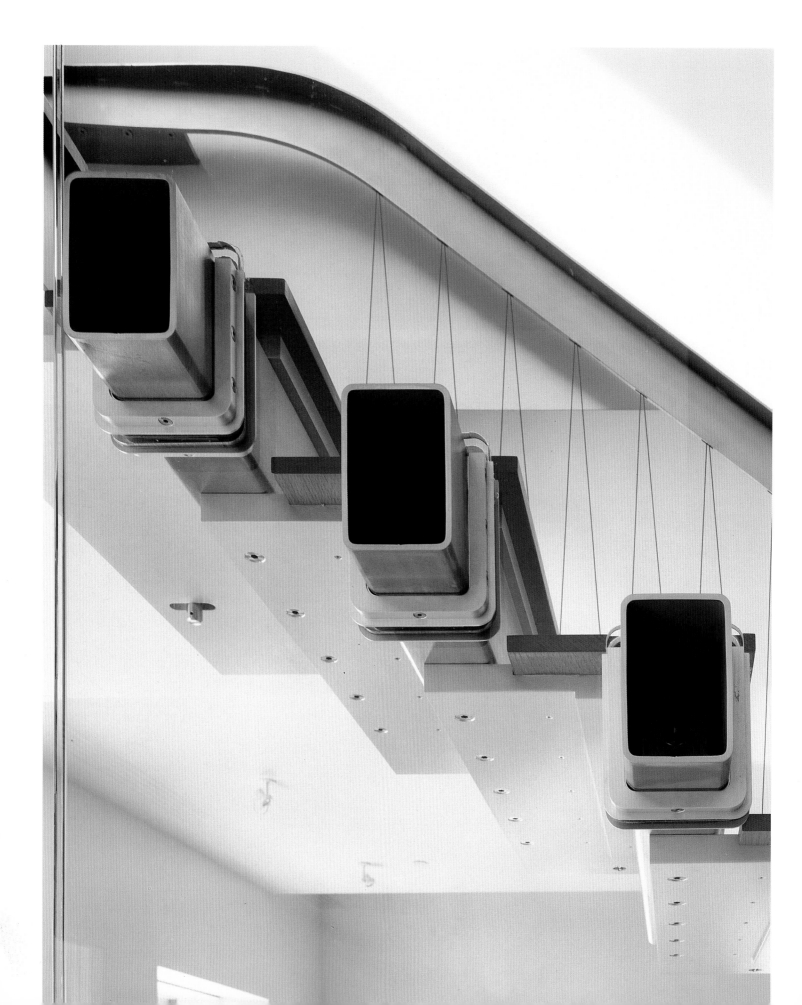

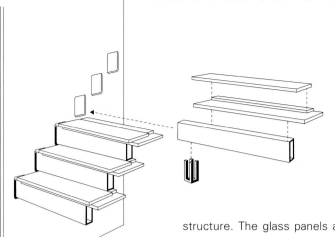

Detail of staircase assembly

major components: two 1.5 x 3.35m (5 x 11ft) panels of 38mm (1½in) thick, water-jet-cut glass, and a stringerless metal and wood stair assembly. Each glass panel is composed of one internal 19mm (¾in) thick tempered-glass sheet and is laminated with two additional 10mm (⅜in) thick tempered-glass sheets. The internal layer resists torsional stresses and makes a conventional stringer unnecessary, enhancing the lightness of the structure. The glass panels are laminated to strengthen the structure and hold the stair assembly together in the event of failure of the internal glass layer.

All the glass panels have water-jet-cut 127 x 178mm (5 x 7in) holes that match the rise and run of the stair assembly and receive tubular risers. The stair itself is composed of 100 x 152mm (4 x 6in) stainless-steel tube risers fastened to anodized aluminium subtreads. The milled aluminium U-brackets and Delrin wedges provide a snug connection between the riser tubes and the bearing surface of the interior glass cutouts. Given the manufacturing tolerances in the glass fabrication, the plastic wedges also allow for adjustment between the two components. White oak treads are fixed to the aluminium subtreads of the stair to create stable walking surfaces. The oak treads, together with a sculptural handrail of stainless steel, soften the powerful geometry of the staircase.

The stair appears to be a cantilevered structure, but this is deceptive: risers are connected to one another, so that the load cascades down the steps and onto the floor. The glass wall, thin as it is, resists the torsion created by the cascading load. The second riser from the floor sits free of the glass plane, relieving the torsion in the glass created by the risers above it. To ensure structural integrity, stress tests were first computer-modelled and then verified on a full-size mock-up to determine the maximum loads on the glass.

The glass wall of the staircase serves as one of several vertical planes designed to establish distinct but interconnected spaces. Planes are made from steel, glass or granite. A blackened steel wall at the entrance of the loft, its patina protected by a wax finish, is punctuated by a massive pivoting entry door. Separated from the living spaces, the master bedroom sits behind a translucent glass wall, which forms one side of the double-height atrium. A heroically scaled partition wall of blue Bahia granite divides the dining area from the kitchen. These materials react to light in different ways, depending on the time of day and location of the sun.

left *The ends of the risers are slotted into precut holes in the glass wall. Although thin, the glass wall resists the torsion created by the cascading load of the stair.*

right *The glass wall of the staircase is as one of several vertical planes designed to establish distinct yet interconnected spaces.*

Presented with a series of commissions in Japan, the Richard Rogers Partnership has taken advantage of ambitious and enlightened clients to engage in formal and spatial experiments that would be virtually impossible to carry out in the West. Although conforming to the constraints of a standard commercial brief, each project has been used as a vehicle for technical innovation, notably in the area of exposed steelwork. In Japan,

RICHARD ROGERS
KABUKI-CHO TOWER, TOKYO, 1993

right *Dramatically poised in space, the steel stair has a bold, industrial quality. Thin treads of perforated metal are supported by the simple tubular steel structure.*

below *The Kabuki-cho tower in its urban context. Circulation elements are pulled clear of the office block itself and the escape stair clings to the concrete lift shaft.*

steel is rarely used in an external structural context, largely because of stringent national building codes, but also because of an inherent conservatism that is fostered by reliance on standard construction packages available off-the-peg from suppliers. In fact, the Kabuki-cho tower required a special dispensation from the Japanese Construction Ministry for its use of exposed steelwork.

The tower occupies a site in one of Tokyo's more colourful, *yakusa-* (gangster) dominated districts. The urban landscape is typically dense and jumbled, full of narrow alleyways lined with bars, all within sight of the skyscrapers of Shinjuku. Hemmed in between a nondescript modern office block and a traditional Japanese villa, the site itself is exceedingly compact. The building contains ten storeys of offices, each floor a compact rectangle of maximized lettable space. In a well-rehearsed reprise of a favourite Rogers device, services and circulation areas are pulled out to the edge of the building to articulate its mass. Yellow washroom modules are neatly stacked up like a child's blocks beside a concrete lift shaft, creating a dominant vertical element. The floors are served by a lift and a fire-escape stair, as is conventional, but in the case of the stair, notions of utility take a dramatic and vertiginous turn.

Somewhat dauntingly for potential users, the escape stair is fully exposed on the outside of the building, suspended from the lift shaft by a network of stainless-steel rods attached to the outer half-landings. Each flight of stairs is pinned to the face of the shaft, creating the effect of a braced cantilever. Treads of very thin perforated metal are supported by a simple tubular steel structure, which is painted bright blue in vivid contrast with the yellow washroom blocks. The entire structure

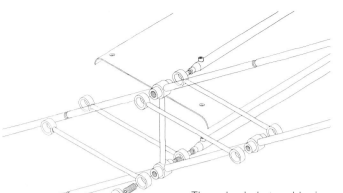

Detail of staircase assembly

has a heroic industrial quality, not unlike an oil rig beached incongruously in the centre of Tokyo.

Despite the prevailing industrial imagery, the detailing of the staircase nonetheless displays a refinement that reflects Rogers' characteristic preoccupation with the way in which things are made and put together. The closely spaced perforations on the treads give the stair structure an enhanced lightness and curious delicacy. They also help to add grip, particularly important in an external situation such as this where the stairs are subject to the random effects of weather. The extreme thinness of the steel plate used to form the treads gives each flight the crisp appearance of a sheet of folded paper. The balustrade is equally finely detailed. Steel flat sections painted black support a simple steel handrail. Two horizontal tensile wires strung tautly between the uprights provide a minimal infill. All this serves to add to the sense of vertiginousness for users, but the stair is only for emergency use and has been meticulously calculated to withstand the most rigorous loading conditions. Towering above the ground, its elegant economy of form and materials demonstrates the way in which High Tech architecture has evolved from its early industrial origins into a sophisticated synthesis of design and construction. Richard Rogers' investigations in this field have always proved stimulating and they still continue to bear fascinating fruit.

Rogers' concern with the autonomy of structure and services accounts for the repeated employment of tension structures, designed in collaboration with the engineering firm Ove Arup & Partners. Tension structures are considerably lighter than equivalent conventional internal structures. Visual mass and internal volume are both minimized, reducing costs and construction time. Structure is designed as a kit of parts, with pin joints, masts, rods, ties, connections and precisely calibrated steel components assembled off-site in ideal factory conditions, and easily erected on site with a minimal amount of site welding and labour-intensive activity. Such an approach generates both flexibility and tectonic refinement.

Local planning controls had stipulated that the Kabuki-cho building should be set back to the rear of the site, creating a large open area facing out on to the street. This has been hewn out and covered by a sloping glass roof, which brings light down to the two floors of offices that are below ground. The roof of the four-storey building is supported by a series of lightweight steel bowstring trusses linked together by tension wires. The deceptive delicacy of the components belies a precisely engineered capability to withstand the extreme loadings that are periodically generated by local typhoon and seismic activity, which is a characteristic of the region. Kabuki-cho is an expressive and pioneering synthesis of structure and materials. Western architects working in Japan have often been engaged specifically to produce signature buildings that usually end up being predictable exercises in attention-seeking. Here, by intelligently challenging existing convention, Rogers has made an invigorating and quite possibly pioneering contribution to the fractured Tokyo cityscape.

left *Each flight of stairs is pinned to the lift shaft, creating the effect of a braced cantilever. Together, the building and staircase are an expressive and inventive synthesis of structure and materials.*

33

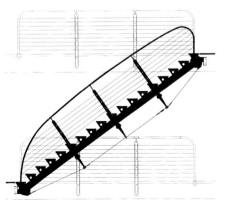

Long section through staircase

above *Constructed from a prefabricated kit of parts, the custom-designed form of the staircase has a spare, engineered elegance.*

right *Detail of tie rods, which combine with the aluminium stringers and legs to form trusses that support the stair.*

When Nicholas Grimshaw & Partners moved to new offices in a former belt factory off Fitzroy Square in London, they found a warren of gloomy cellular rooms. The six-storey building has since been converted into a light, airy *atelier*, humming with life. A steel frame replaces the the need for internal load-bearing walls and partitions have been removed to transform each floor into a single open space. Both industrial and urbane, it suits an architect's

NICHOLAS GRIMSHAW
OFFICES, LONDON, 1992

office, which, according to Grimshaw, is "a cross between a workshop, studio, office and manufacturing plant."

Embodying Grimshaw's approach to design and detailing, the new central stair is a focal element in the offices. Both visitors and staff use it and its sleek, sculptural form is also highly visible from the street. Made predominantly of aluminium, it is light and open, which allows daylight to penetrate and eliminates the need for complex construction operations. In fact, it was assembled by hand when the offices were already in use and carried into place by Grimshaw and his staff. In its spare, engineered elegance, it demonstrates Grimshaw's fondness for prefabrication – the parts were made to exacting tolerances to preclude on-site drilling and welding – as well as for creatively combining available materials and the selective use of custom-designed elements.

The stair's stringers are off-the-peg mast sections with the supports for the treads slotted and locked into the sail grooves. At either end of each flight, cast-aluminium "fish heads" are clamped to the stringers to form end bearings. At the mid-span, cast "legs" are fixing points for stainless-steel tie-rods, reinforcing the exceptionally lightweight structure. These thin rods combine with the aluminium stringers and legs to form trusses that support the stairs.

above *Detail of perforated steel tread. Supports for the treads are slotted and locked into grooves in the stringers, which are made from sections of yacht masts.*

Specialist fabricators produced various parts of the stair. The aluminium components were made from standard sections without welding, castings were bead-blasted after machining, and the tie-rods and rod connectors were supplied by a yacht-rigging manufacturer. Once the stair had been assembled, the perforated steel treads were fixed in place, each flight lifted into position and the fish heads secured to supporting beams. Finally, the slim tubular aluminium handrails were attached and rigged. The outcome is an unqualified success and the practice is considering introducing a third flight to join the existing two.

When the pop group the Pet Shop Boys (consisting of Chris Lowe and Neil Tennant) decided to establish a new headquarters in west London, Alan Brookes was commissioned to redesign the top floor of a converted garage to create an office and informal studio space in which to relax and listen to music. Exploiting the existing split-level arrangement, the studio was located on the upper entrance level, with the offices 1.5m (5ft) below. An

ALAN BROOKES
CHRIS LOWE OFFICES, LONDON, 1990

exquisitely detailed curved stair links the two levels. Drawing its inspiration from traditional Japanese bridges, the stair arcs gracefully through the simple, uncluttered space.

A thick storage wall frames the office entrance. This connects through to the large bare studio room, which is sparsely furnished with Biedermeier chairs and a long glass shelf on which state-of-the-art music equipment is reverentially displayed as if in a gallery. The office beneath the studio is equally austere, with bare white walls and minimal furniture. The calm spaces act as a neutral canvas to the focal point of the interior, the curved linking staircase. Designed as an eye-catching free-standing object, it resembles a piece of contemporary sculpture or furniture. With its shallow steel risers and lightly supported single handrail, it exudes a sense of weightlessness and spare refinement.

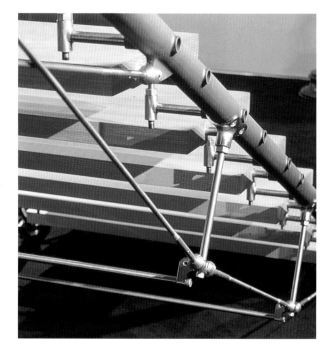

The stair is fundamentally a pair of curved steel tubes 48mm (1⅞in) in diameter connected by 40mm (1½in) thick treads made from solid ash. Tubes and treads are united into a single structure by a lattice of thin stainless-steel tension rods. The treads are held in place by specially designed adjustable steel support pads. Steel pins are dowelled into the treads from the support pads and also from the curved stringer tubes. This arrangement ensures that there is no bending at the joints, giving the compact structure an elegant clarity. Minimally supported at just four points along the stair, the slim single handrail is made from a steel tube 20mm (¾in) in diameter. Both ends of the stringer tubes rest on stainless-steel rocker bearings, so the stair is entirely independent from the rest of the building. This effectively resolves the different angles of contact in one detail and means that the stair could be easily relocated if necessary.

Apart from its obvious resemblance to traditional Japanese bridges, this beautifully curved staircase also evokes comparisons with musical instruments: it literally rings as people walk up and down its length, with the result that the tranquil office and studio spaces are sporadically infused with a strange, lyrical resonance.

above *Detail of staircase treads and stringers. Curved steel tubes form the stringers, connected by treads of solid ash. Tubes and treads are joined by a lattice of stainless-steel tension rods.*

above *Curving lithely from a gallery space down to offices, the stair appears light and refined.*

Long section through staircase

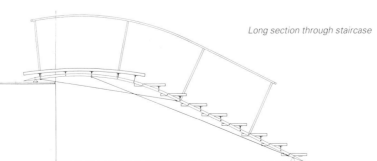

Eva Jiricna was commissioned to refurbish a Knightsbridge apartment that occupies the lower half of a Victorian terraced house, overlooking a typical London square. Having already lost all its period features in a previous conversion, the apartment could be gutted and conceived anew. Originally, it was divided into two apartments on three floors, connected by an external staircase. As part of a general scheme for unifying the

EVA JIRICNA
KNIGHTSBRIDGE APARTMENT, LONDON, 1992

left *In a lyrical fusion of engineering and architecture, the glittering cascade of glass treads is suspended from a stainless-steel mesh balustrade. Light percolates through the delicate lattice of steel and glass.*

apartment, a new internal stair was required, for which Jiricna suggested a spectacular steel and glass spiral that would explore a similar language to her famous stairs for the Joseph chain (see pages 22–5). The client, a collector of art and antiques, had originally wanted a traditional interior, but an appreciation of art fuelled his interest in Jiricna's radical modern proposal.

Forming the apartment's centrepiece, the new staircase is a *tour de force* of both architecture and engineering. Consuming the minimum of space, the staircase has a transparency that allows light to filter around the house. It is beguilingly translucent and glittering, yet reassuringly solid. Spiralling up through the building, it resembles a shining steel and glass beanstalk and its structure, like that of a plant, satisfies both functional and structural imperatives in the most economical fashion.

The main supporting system of the staircase is based on a lattice of balustrading formed of slim steel rods and ties, connected without the need for welding by means of "sweated" joints. This creates a strong, rigid external beam, from which the thin glass treads are suspended. The central newel is formed from a 30cm (12in) diameter steel tube, which has been reduced to a ribbon-like spiral running from top to bottom. The newel is sprayed with silvery-grey metallic paint. Treads of 19mm (¾in) thick glass on 15mm (⁹⁄₁₆in) acrylic sheet are fixed at three points and sandblasted with a scintillating diamond pattern, which diffuses light through the delicate structure. The finely judged combination of the lacy balustrading and glass treads has a seductive, sparkling intensity.

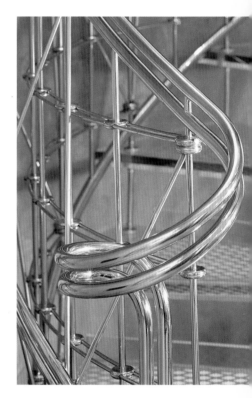

above *Detail of the sinuous stainless-steel handrail and balustrade. The elegant steel rods and ties for the balustrade are connected together by means of "sweated" joints.*

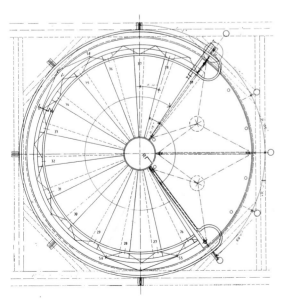

Plan of typical staircase flight

Surrounding spaces are resolved with a characteristically light touch, allowing Jiricna to concentrate all her energies on the technical complexity of the stair. Gradations of grey in different textures – from gleaming steel to smooth plaster and the variegated grey of stone floors – visually unify the various spaces. As with her stair in the Joseph shop, the interiors form a neutral backdrop to the focal stair. Here Jiricna uses an architectural language that accommodates the quotidian and the conventional without sacrificing the architecture's rigour or expressive power.

The great Italian rationalist architect Gio Ponti once wrote that in a house, stairs are "the abstract, non-domestic element, a geometry measured by the compass of paces, by our legs". Perhaps precisely because of this non-domestic character, Eva Jiricna has elevated the staircase to be the compelling central focus of this domestic design, developing a compositional theme of which she is particularly fond. Yet given the size of the site and the type of building (long and narrow and spread over different levels), vertical circulation logically assumes a crucial importance. The outcome is that the house is totally transfixed by its steel and glass staircase, as precious and glittering as a piece of jewellery. The conspicuously expressive mood matches the lightness of design and the ethereality of materials, which are further disembodied by the way in which light shines through them.

As in previous staircase designs in which she opts for a duet of steel and glass, Jiricna relishes the materials' exactness of detail while simultaneously contorting them into soft, supple and almost organic forms. The stair is transformed into a kind of sculpture, created by assembling glass blades and steel curves around a sinuous central ribbon. In this way she achieves an unusual richness of expression from these traditionally unresponsive and not inherently decorative materials, while at the same time avoiding any redundancy of line or formal excess. Intriguingly, the staircase closely resembles the actual drawings of its geometric construction, as if it were a direct transcription of a graphic representation, with lines transposed into metal patterns.

Jiricna has created an interior where the dominant role assigned to the "stair room" is offset by the reductivist character of the spaces surrounding it. Characteristically, this is achieved by unifying materials and colour as well as by minimizing the amount of furniture. In this contrast between the subdued and subtle tone of the design as a whole and the expressive spotlighting of the staircase, Jiricna's design approach is explicit: she concentrates on the technically and figuratively more complex elements and solves the others simply, with a deft touch.

right *The staircase spirals upwards to a graceful conclusion in the living space. The ribbon-like central newel extends further to form a dynamic sculptural element.*

below *The glass treads are sandblasted with a scintillating diamond pattern to assist grip. The entire structure shimmers and glistens with a seductive intensity.*

By the end of the 1980s, the European Court of Human Rights, one of the highest courts in Europe, had outgrown its original headquarters and plans for a new building in Strasbourg were well advanced – to the extent that France's President Mitterrand had been invited to lay the foundation stone. However, an extraordinary volte-face occurred. On reviewing the proposals, Mitterrand pointedly refused to undertake the ceremony and decreed that the

RICHARD ROGERS
EUROPEAN COURT OF HUMAN RIGHTS, STRASBOURG. 1995

design should be put out to competition. Out of a democratically representative quartet of European architects (O.M. Ungers, Rafael Moneo, Dominique Perrault and Richard Rogers), the commission was eventually awarded to Richard Rogers, who intended the building to be a "non-monumental monument", a dignified yet accessible expression of the role of the law in modern European society. The resulting building has an openness that is both metaphorical and literal (although, in reality, the public are unable to penetrate far beyond the courts and entrance hall) and, unlike many of its neighbours, it has a clarity of intent and organization that can only serve to enhance its institutional role.

Each function of the institution has a discrete area of the building, which is arranged in a vaguely zoomorphic pattern of head, neck and tail. The bug-eyed head consists of two chamfered cylinders linked by an intermediate glass drum. The brilliant engineer Peter Rice, who worked closely with the Rogers team on the project before his death in 1993, played an instrumental role in resolving the complex geometrical interrelationship of the three circular volumes. The main meeting chambers and support spaces are arranged along the short axis of the building leading directly to the offices along the river. The larger of the cylinders houses the building's symbolic and functional focus, the European Court of Human Rights. The smaller one is occupied by the European Commission. Although used only intermittently, the chambers are the set-piece performance spaces around which, in the manner of a theatre, the rest of the building revolves. Beyond the bulbous head is a narrow neck containing meeting spaces; beyond this, entomological metaphors give way to nautical ones, as the two stepped, parallel office blocks curve along the bank of the River Ill, like a great ocean-going liner. A landscaped open space with pools and fountains occupies the elongated

above *The curved staircase winds up to a suspended mezzanine level, that gives access to the courtrooms. Materials and detailing reflect Rogers' interest in industrial functionalism.*

above *The central hall is the building's social focus. The staircase is conceived as a leisurely promenade up to the mezzanine level, its blue structure in vivid contrast to the red mezzanine steelwork.*

43

courtyard between the two office wings. As more nations sign up to the Council of Europe, the office tailpiece can simply be extended incrementally along the river.

Rogers' intention to demystify the processes of law is perhaps most potently realized in the pivotal entrance hall that links the two chambers. Instead of the sometimes daunting claustrophobia often associated with law courts, he has created a magically transparent drum, full of light, spatial drama and tectonic intricacy.

Suspended between the two chambers is a doughnut-shaped mezzanine, linked to the lower level of the entrance hall by a gently curving staircase. The stair consists of two flights with an intermediate landing, which is suspended by slim tensile rods from the main steel structure of the mezzanine. Each flight is supported by a central spine composed of a curved tubular steel truss. Epitomizing a familiar Rogers aesthetic of quasi-industrial materials animated by scintillating bursts of colour, the vivid blue stair structure forms a bold contrast with the red mezzanine steelwork, which in turn contrasts with the exposed fair-faced concrete finish of the drums housing the courts. Beyond the building's industrial functionalism, there are also references to Russian Constructivism in the red metalwork of the lift shafts and rooftop plant rooms.

Conceived as a languid, ceremonial promenade up to the mezzanine level, the entrance hall stair is generously proportioned, with a shallow riser height to ease ascent and descent. It also has a surprising delicacy. Treads made of thin sheets of translucent glass diffuse light through the structure. These are held in place by steel brackets connected to the tubular spinal truss. Steel strips fixed to the long edges of the treads form protective nosings to minimize daily wear and tear. Cantilevered out from the spinal trusses, thin steel balusters support infill panels of clear glass topped by an elegant curved tubular steel handrail. Poised above the transparent balustrade, the handrail appears to float in thin air. In the luminous volume of the entrance hall, the winding, weightless stair is an embodiment of Rogers' constantly inventive appropriation of materials and construction technology.

left *Appearing elegant and weightless, the curved stair hangs in space. Treads are made of thin sheets of translucent glass supported by steel brackets attached to a tubular spinal steel truss.*

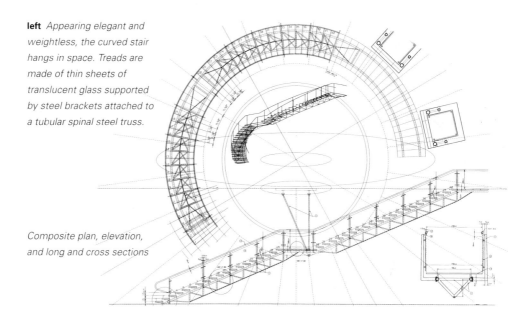

Composite plan, elevation, and long and cross sections

One of the most distinctive British contributions to architecture over the last decade is an enthusiasm for improvisation. Architects such as Norman Foster, Eva Jiricna and Future Systems share a common preference for inventive and complex customized design solutions over conventional off-the-peg alternatives. Few exemplify this approach more than John Young, an architect who has worked with Richard Rogers since the days of the

JOHN YOUNG
THAMES REACH PENTHOUSE, LONDON, 1991

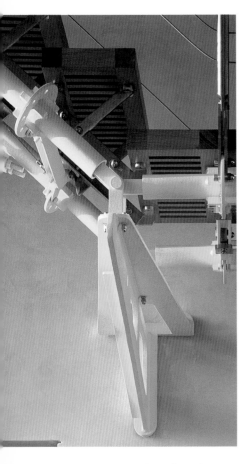

above *A smaller staircase links the sleeping loft with the roof terraces. It shares with the main stair its nautical-industrial detailing and its bold use of colour.*

Pompidou Centre in Paris, an early iconic High Tech building, which, with its services and structure brazenly displayed on its exterior, celebrates the potential of construction. Young delights in creating mechanisms of extraordinary ingenuity, as demonstrated by the highly unconventional staircase in his London apartment.

Young's penthouse beside the River Thames is carved out of two units of a residential block, itself designed by the Rogers partnership. Inspired by lighthouses, airships, Ferris wheels and industrial structures, Young's version of architecture has little to do with devising elegant floor plans or manipulating space to create a sense of progression and order. There are few conventional signs of domesticity, and bedroom, bathroom, kitchen and staircase have all been used as points of departure for Young's maverick, mechanically inspired extemporizations.

The apartment is structured around three elements. The first is the river outside, which fills the interior with luminous reflections and changing waterscapes. The second is the sheer quantity of space inside this lofty urban eyrie – the main living area is a huge, double-height space. The third is the jewel-like quality of the carefully crafted insertions scattered around the interior.

Young sourced many details from other fields, such as the maritime and aeronautical industries. The floors, like the decks of boats, are laid in teak and the chunky floodlights that serve as light fittings are appropriated from Italian studio photography equipment. Wall-mounted platecoil heaters arranged like vertical rows of dustbin lids were supplied by a Texan manufacturer of heat ranges for industrial appliances. Metal kitchen cabinets and storage units are finished in a moiré pattern which has been copied from Japanese delivery trucks.

above *The main staircase leading up to the sleeping loft arcs athletically through the tall living space. The bow of the truss generates a variable tread-to-rise ratio, with the staircase becoming nearly horizontal towards the top.*

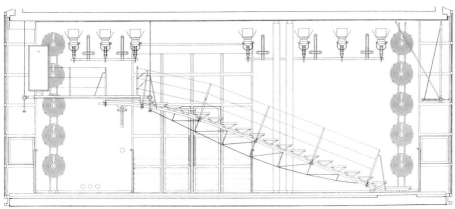

*Long section through sleeping
loft and staircase*

above *Detail of the base of the main staircase, which resembles a ship's gangplank. Teak treads are supported on profiled steel brackets attached to a stainless-steel carriage. The slender cable balustrade continues the nautical imagery.*

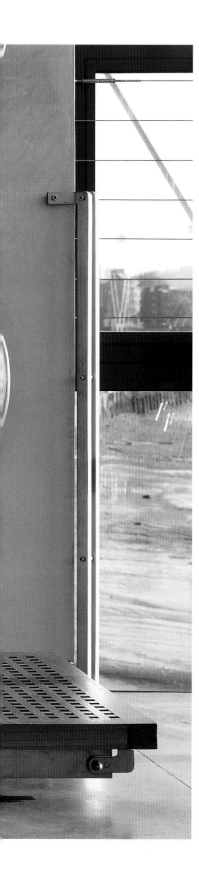

The master bedroom is a loft suspended over the living room by a series of slender stainless-steel rods. Hoisting the bedroom up in this way creates a fluid transition between living, eating and sleeping areas. Access to the loft is by means of an intricately constructed stair, which, resembling a giant piece of Meccano, is fabricated from steel, timber and tensile wires. The staircase forms one of the apartment's key elements and presented Young with a particularly fertile opportunity to improvise.

The stair gently arcs through the living room supported by curved steel trusses that are painted canary yellow, a signature Rogers colour that exudes confidence and optimism. A stainless-steel carriage rests on the curved trusses, to which the treads are attached by profiled stainless-steel supports. The treads are pieces of teak 50mm (2in) thick, polished and sealed, with a gridded pattern punched into the surface. A delicate balustrade is formed from stainless-steel cables 4mm (⅛in) in diameter, which are strung horizontally through tubular steel stanchions. The bow of the truss generates a variable tread-to-rise ratio, so that, as it reaches the top, the stair becomes almost horizontal. At the base, the stair bears on small wheels like those of a gangplank.

A secondary staircase links the sleeping loft with a roof terrace. This shares the same proto-industrial language and detailing, but is narrower than the main stair and straight in profile instead of bowed.

With its evocative celebration of industrial imagery, Young's apartment has strong echoes of Jean Prouvé's radical, functional buildings and Pierre Chareau's Maison de Verre in Paris. (Young's elegant cylindrical bath tower in the penthouse is made from translucent glass blocks in a witty homage to the latter.) Architects such as Prouvé and Chareau pushed construction methods and materials to extremes, and, like Young, produced work characterized by a density of detail that generates its own, very particular aesthetic. Never opting for the easiest solution, Young's penthouse is a proving ground for testing and refining ideas about construction technology. The cavernous space acts as a neutral backdrop for a series of ingenious explorations into how things are made and put together. And, in designing the focal staircase, Young was at pains to make a clear distinction between the load-bearing elements and the stainless-steel carriage that supports the teak steps. This urge for clarity has generated a fascinating intricacy of detail – perhaps, as Young has subsequently admitted, it is slightly over-complex, but the effect is entirely admirable nonetheless. The staircase transforms the simple act of going upstairs to bed into a dramatic domestic ritual.

above *In its boldly expressed constructional intricacy the staircase resembles a giant piece of Meccano. Bowed steel trusses painted yellow form stringers.*

The name Future Systems has become synonymous with a particular kind of architecturally pioneering and creative design. Founded in 1979 by Czech-born Jan Kaplicky, the practice designs modern, organic forms that used to be seen as visionary but impractical. This is no longer the case, as a steady stream of recent projects shows. With his provocative ideas and buildings, Kaplicky continues a tradition of talented European

FUTURE SYSTEMS
HAUER-KING HOUSE, LONDON, 1994

above *Detail of the aluminium spine beam stiffened with stainless-steel wire that forms the stair's structural support.*

left *Fabricated from an efficient and meticulously calculated kit of parts, the staircase in the house's entrance lobby rises up three storeys.*

émigrés making an influential contribution to the British architectural scene. At a time when most architects prefer to embrace the safety of the past, his compelling images make possible a new belief in the creative potential of a technologically based architecture.

Investigating the possibilities of different building technologies has always been a key preoccupation for Future Systems; in fact it runs like a thread through their projects. They have embraced the lightness and strength of aircraft construction together with the compactness and performance of automobile design, striving to achieve the aesthetic of the efficient machine. Future Systems' projects also reflect the influence of the radical, pioneering inventiveness of twentieth-century Czech architecture and industrial design, which so inspired Jan Kaplicky during his early years in Prague.

Future Systems' first commission was a temporary hospitality tent for the Museum of the Moving Image on London's South Bank. This was followed by an exhibition at the Royal Institute of British Architects in 1991, which helped to raise the practice's profile. From this came a commission from restaurateur Jeremy King and his wife Debra Hauer to design a remarkable private family house. Located in Canonbury, north London, the house is squeezed between a nineteenth-century pub and a Georgian terrace. Its four-storey-high street frontage is composed entirely of glass blocks and is accessed by a curved steel and aluminium walkway. To the rear, a glass wall slopes down at an angle of 50 degrees, enveloping the house in a shimmering transparent membrane. Comprising twenty-two panels of thermally efficient, silicone-sealed double glazing, the dramatically cascading glass wall gives the house's occupants not so much an unimpeded view of the outside world, as the illusion of actually living in the air.

The house's living space is divided into four decks that reduce in size towards the top of the building. The largest and lowest of these consists of a kitchen and dining space backed up by a spare bedroom and a utility room on the north side. Above is a first floor, which is actually the entrance level, containing a tall entrance lobby, a storage wall, and a living area overlooking the dining space below. Bedrooms occupy the two upper floors. The house contains two staircases: a single flight links the ground-floor kitchen with the living room above, while a double flight runs up through the three-storey entrance lobby. The arrangement of the latter stair makes it possible for the side walls of the entrance hall to be used as bookcases and shelves.

Both stairs are of identical design and form. In effect, they are formed from an efficient and carefully calculated kit of parts. Tubular aluminium handrails are supported by cantilevered treads, which are carried by elliptical-section extruded aluminium beams that are stiffened with stainless-steel rigging wire. Like a spine, the aluminium beams run down the centre of each stair. (Typically of the multi-functionality of so many of this house's components, a beam fabricated from sections of the same elliptical aluminium extrusion is used to support the back of the house's angled glass wall at its mid-point.)

The steps of both of the staircases were formed from extremely thin sheets of aluminium (a mere 6mm [¼in] thick), which were then simply bent in two to form a composite tread and riser. The highly polished surface of the aluminium has a subtle, silvery sheen and is engraved with four grooves along the nosing of each tread to ensure a good grip.

Between the aluminium rails at the top and bottom of the balustrade, intermediate safety cords of tensionable white nylon are strung horizontally through stainless-steel stanchions like the strings of a musical instrument. Continuing the theme of multi-functionality, the same handrail and balustrade detail, with its tension cord safety net, is used for all the transverse stairs and landings and also for the balcony balustrading at the edge of the first-floor slab.

Combining a sense of weightlessness and transparency with ingenious detailing and construction, the Hauer-King staircases astutely reconcile old functional design principles with the evolving world of material and technological possibilities. The house is a *tour de force*, but not one laden with heroic structural and mechanical bravado. Rather, it is an intriguing synthesis of time-honoured and innovative elements that conspire to generate an extraordinary spectacle. Its glacial transparency and futuristic form are rendered all the more remarkable by its setting in a leafy London borough, surrounded by reminders of the city's Georgian and Victorian past.

above *Balustrades are infilled with tensionable white nylon cords like the strings of a musical instrument. The same detail is repeated on all the flights.*

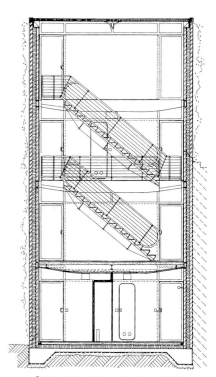

Cross section through entrance lobby

right *The staircase is an imposing presence in the tall, narrow volume of the entrance hall. Treads and risers are made of thin aluminium sheet carried on the spinal beams.*

Since the mid-1980s, Eva Jiricna has designed more than thirty glass staircases in a variety of settings, including stores, houses and nightclubs. Staircases provide her with the opportunity for apparently endless innovative variations on a theme. Each presents a new challenge in terms of functional constraints such as client requirements, geometry, admitting light into dark areas and reducing construction time on site. She manages to

EVA JIRICNA
JOAN & DAVID STORE, LONDON, 1995

cope brilliantly with such pragmatic concerns, and for sheer delight there are few architectural experiences to match a Jiricna staircase. Through her subtle handling of light, illusion and transparency, the experience of vertical circulation is elevated into a feast for the senses. For the Joseph store in Fulham Road, London, designed in the late 1980s, a steel and glass staircase leads down from the women's floor to the men's. The brightly lit and sparkling cage, suspended on stainless-steel hangers from the underside of the first floor, has an exuberant, theatrical glamour, heralding the emergence of a singular approach to staircase design that fused art and engineering in an astonishing alliance. This original straight staircase has since metamorphosed into a spiral; initially on a domestic scale, where it penetrated and unified three floors of a nineteenth-century house in Knightsbridge (see pages 38–41), and more recently for a sumptuous shoe emporium in the heart of the West End.

In the early 1990s, Jiricna was commissioned to provide a new interior of appropriately understated elegance for the upmarket American Joan & David shoe store in London's New Bond Street. Having worked with the owners since the late 1980s, Jiricna has built up a strong relationship with the firm, which, like Joseph Ettedgui, has become a loyal and discriminating patron of her designs. Her first Joan & David design, for a concession in the Harvey Nichols department store in London, was followed by work in some fifty or more stores, mostly in North America, but increasingly also in Europe. The Bond Street store was the first dedicated Joan & David outlet in the UK.

The store occupies the ground and basement floors of former Ireland House on a prominent corner site. While acknowledging the context, Jiricna's design strives to

above *In an almost intuitive synthesis of strength and lightness, glass treads are cantilevered from a central spiral mild-steel stringer on stainless-steel brackets.*

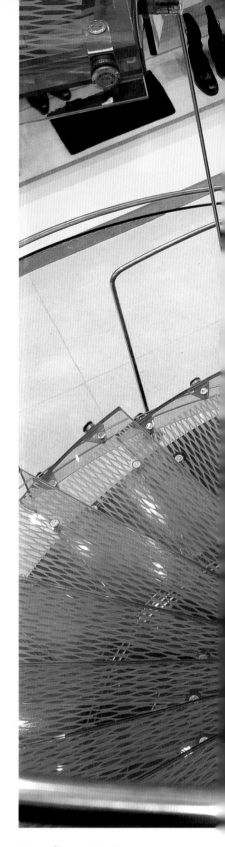

above *Glass and steel catch and reflect the light, transforming the stair into a lustrous, sparkling jewel at the heart of the store.*

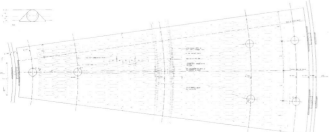

Plan of staircase tread

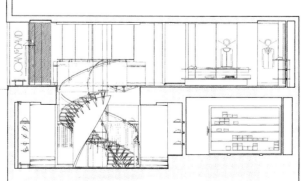

Cross section through store

create an interior oasis that is screened from the blare of the traffic yet also permits glimpses inside. The original interior elements were stripped out, save for the columns, to create simple plans on both levels featuring a single clear space for circulation with shelving set around the perimeter. This is supplemented by a handful of free-standing units for display and sales. The main New Bond Street frontage is fully glazed, while on the Bruton Street façade a fretted timber screen runs behind the window display which affords a degree of privacy for customers while allowing oblique views into the store.

The existing staircase was demolished, establishing a strong central axis on the ground floor from the entrance on New Bond Street to the rear wall and sales counter. The new stair, which has been moved to one side of the store, is a spiralling version of Jiricna's famous steel and glass confections. A curved spine wall clad in steel panels supports the glass treads by means of mild-steel outriggers held in polished stainless-steel brackets. Delicate triangular brackets hold the treads above the central spine wall in such a way that they appear to float. Treads are linked to paired rods by bosses, which also hold the balustrade in position. Formed from curved panels of toughened glass, the balustrade is topped by a slim stainless-steel handrail. Floor-to-ceiling tension rods provide additional stiffness for the composite structure.

The jewel-like glass treads are sandblasted with an intricate diamond pattern. The glass catches and reflects spotlights embedded in the ceiling above, so that the entire structure glimmers, an effect intensified by sheets of reflecting glass set around the base of the staircase. A glass landing at ground-floor level emphasizes the transparency of the staircase structure and enhances the visual connection between the two levels of the store.

Throughout, handling of materials and detailing is restrained – a backdrop for the complex constructional fireworks of the staircase. Floors are of honey-coloured stone laid in square tiles, set off by the warm stained maple of the furniture and screens. On the ground floor, a fretted wooden screen on the Bruton Street elevation filters light and views to and from the street. The screen alternates with timber doors to the store windows and curves into a solid wall to soften a corner. Undulating lines of cantilevered glass shelving lit by concealed lighting heighten the sense of ephemerality. On the

above *With its calm, muted hues and restrained use of materials, the interior of the store is conceived as a neutral backdrop for the constructional pyrotechnics of the spiral staircase.*

above *The glass treads are sandblasted with a diamond pattern, adding to the glittering effect. The curved glass balustrade is exquisitely minimal, rounded off with a slender stainless-steel handrail.*

ceiling, pinprick spotlights bathe spaces in a soft Italianate glow, giving a far more refined and sensuous impression than the glittery set dressings often contrived in the name of luxury.

"Doing more with less" has been a constant theme of modern architecture, a way of achieving a formal economy that exudes both dignity and delight. The Japanese describe this as *kinari*, a traditional aesthetic based on unadorned beauty and a tenet that has had a

MINIMAL ELEGANCE

profound influence on generations of Western architects. The quest for ascetic refinement finds contemporary expression in many ways, but more recently, traditional Japanese influences have been evident in the development of an austerely minimal approach to design. This espouses a language of simple forms and finely honed materials to generate architecture and interiors that have an elemental potency.

It appears effortless, but requires both skill and tenacity. In architecture, where elements must be designed and produced separately, yet fit together as though they were parts of a single organism, the semblance of simplicity is achieved by discipline and attention to detail. The epitome of such achievement is the staircase, which paradoxically can be a highly complex element in its planning and construction. It must conform to countless regulations governing fire and safety, yet use materials and methods in a way that is elegant but not extravagant. It represents in microcosm the constant struggle to create something that is both beautiful and functional. Distilling such complexities into staircases of immense formal and material refinement presents a challenge that continues to elicit a diversity of inspiring responses from architects and designers.

Polished materials and elemental forms are combined in this staircase at the Casa Solarium in Biella, Piemonte, designed by Magyar Marsoni Architects.

Commissioned to design a house on a very narrow site in the suburbs of Nijmegen in the Netherlands, Bert Dirrix responded with a model of spatial and material ingenuity. The plot was originally occupied by an elegant 1930s villa, which dictated the extent of any further development. The available building land was a strip measuring a mere 5m (16ft 5in) wide by 28m (92ft) long. The resulting plan is a more or less continuous, elongated space,

BERT DIRRIX
HOUSE, NIJMEGEN, 1997

interspersed with two courtyards incised into the mass of the building. Designed to trap the morning and evening sun, these courtyards bring light into the hermetic volume. To maximize the play of light, all the internal elements are pared down to virtual invisibility.

The house is two storeys high, and in such a situation a dog-leg stair with a half landing would be the usual solution. However the narrow plan could not comfortably accommodate a dog-leg; moreover, an enclosed stairwell would block light transmission. Instead, Dirrix has created a remarkable single-flight staircase that slots neatly into the space, taking up as little room as possible. The staircase is formed from a single strip of galvanized steel just 10mm (⅜in) thick. The strip has been bent and folded to produce a rigid, concertina-like form. In a dazzlingly simple and inventive conceit, the undulations of the strip create the treads and stringers. The folding produces an interrupted outer stringer coupling two treads together, which gives the stair stability despite the relative thinness of the steel plate. The steel concertina is supported on one side only, so that it hangs tantalizingly in space, appearing to defy both gravity and structural logic. Single bolts through the stringers fix the stair to the wall. There is no balustrade on the open side, only a slim tubular steel handrail fixed to the wall on the other, as if in grudging concession to the demands of safety. Yet, despite its defiance of convention, the entire composition has a breathtaking economy and elegance.

By conceiving steps and stringers as a thin folded ribbon, Dirrix achieves a maximum of transparency with the absolute minimum of materials. The stair connects with a landing on the first floor made of industrial steel grating. The open mesh of the landing allows light to filter down through the house, just as the openness of the stair allows unobstructed views through the long space. Despite the stair's apparent precariousness, the house's occupants – a family with two young sons – have risen to the challenge of using it. The minimal quality of the stair is echoed in the employment of sober, raw materials in other parts of the house, amplifying the extreme elementality of Dirrix's approach.

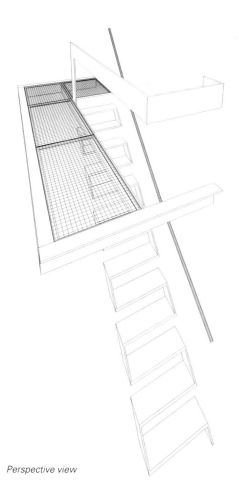

Perspective view

left *Exquisitely minimal so as to occupy as little space as possible and allow light transmission through the house, the staircase is simply a piece of thin galvanized steel folded into a concertina of treads and risers.*

In 1989, Richard Meier was commissioned by the conglomerate Hypobank to design a headquarters for its subsidiary Hypolux in the Kirchberg banking district of Luxembourg. This is a satellite zone without historical precedent or urban context and most buildings turn inward, occupying a full block. Meier, however, introduced a sense of civic space by wrapping his building around an open square. His composition, a characteristically incisive

RICHARD MEIER
HYPOLUX BUILDING, LUXEMBOURG, 1993

above *Subtle contrasts of colour and texture, used here to great effect in the charcoal treads and white balustrade, are a characteristic mark of Meier's work.*

right *The regular grids of both the atrium and the protective cage contrast with the relaxed yet elegant curvature of the stairs.*

above *A glass curtain wall exposes the stair and its protective drum, echoing the cylindrical entrance structure.*

exploration of Euclidean geometry, is based on a four-storey cylindrical building linked to an L-shaped office slab. The crisp white cylinder marks the building entrance, extolling the corporate presence of the bank. The cylinder is a signature Meier device and is reprised on a smaller scale in the sculptural, free-standing spiral staircase that links the four floors of offices together.

The stair, which is the focal element of a tall atrium space adjoining the entrance hall, is contained within a protective cage formed from slim, horizontal steel ribs. The cage provides lateral support for the main stair structure, which spirals languidly upward to connect with a series of open walkways overlooking the atrium. The walkways run longitudinally through the banking offices. Both vertical and horizontal circulation are thus exposed, and the comings and goings of staff and customers animate the space. The curved monolithic skin of the balustrade simply and elegantly encloses the stair, like a coiled wood shaving or furling white ribbon. A delicious tension is orchestrated between the regular grid of the cage and the sensuous, organic sweep of the balustrade. Charcoal carpet on the stair reduces noise and provides a subtle variation on Meier's minimal palette of white-enamelled metal panels and grey Iragna gneiss stone. Directly above the stair, the ceiling is pierced by a cylindrical skylight, focusing daylight on the tower like a spotlight.

More sculpture than functional element, Meier's stair could be mistaken for one of the works of art scattered around the building. The most conspicuous of these is a large installation by Frank Stella that dominates the entrance courtyard. Inspired by the configurations of cooling cigar smoke, Stella's welded confection of antiquated metal contrasts with the sleek purity of the bank building. It could be interpreted as a veiled criticism of the banking business in the same way as Meier's corkscrew staircase might be seen as a metaphor for the screw of financial turnover spiralling interminably upward.

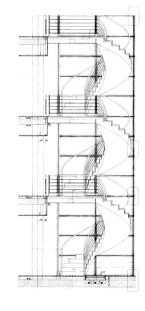

Cross section through staircase

The reality of the artist's studio often differs very little from an ordinary, uncomfortable workshop, yet it is also a place of reverie, a universe apart, a world in itself. A commission for a studio therefore touches at the core of successful architecture, embodying an alchemical combination of the prosaic and the poetic; and it is also a powerful reminder of the way in which original bare matter is transformed into a work of art. So it was with

ERIC PARRY
ARTIST'S STUDIO, LONDON, 1989

some degree of fascination that Eric Parry approached an opportunity to explore the nature of studio space for two very different artists.

Spanning a gap in a terrace of shops in Camberwell, south London, a pair of impressively large, battered steel doors leads into a secret inner realm. This is where painter Tom Philips and sculptor Antony Gormley work. They share a courtyard around which studios have been formed – some new and some carved out of existing structures. Both artists live near the site and it was this, rather than a shared ideological position, that drew them to it. Tom Philips' work is extraordinarily diverse, responsive and consistently exploratory, embracing many disciplines such as painting, poetry and music. Antony Gormley is a sculptor who is almost exclusively concerned with the human body as a source of ideas about humanity and existence. Philips required a studio, printing works and exhibition space, while Gormley needed a versatile studio space that could be used both as a studio, office and workshop, and as somewhere to exhibit his work. Eric Parry was commissioned to provide a solution and his response is intriguing. An artist's existence is paradoxical, being both intensely private and necessarily public, and the studios embody and crystallize the relationship between these two extremes.

Originally a laundry and latterly a garage, the courtyard site consisted of two main buildings, which have been retained, and a group of lean-to structures, now demolished. Each artist occupies one side of the courtyard and the studios are linked by a heavy rusticated brick wall that encloses Gormley's large sculpture workshop.

Tom Philips' studio is a tower inserted into the existing wall, creating a densely planned and vertically organized sequence of spaces. This is the most elaborately considered and detailed part of the building. At ground-floor level, an exhibition space gives access both to a staircase within the tower and beyond to the printing and etching workshop. Evoking the image of the

right Like a flower blossoming and unfolding outward, a beautifully detailed steel staircase links the first-floor reading area with the main studio on the mezzanine above.

Elevation of staircase between first floor and mezzanine level

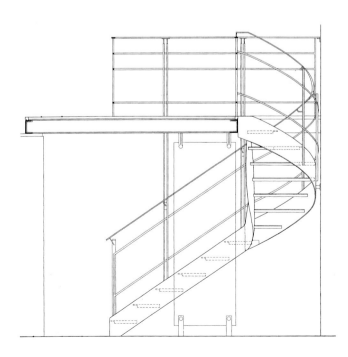

studiolo or Saint Jerome in his study, a reading area overlooks the courtyard and studio. This space is equipped with a raised area for a model and can be used for drawing, painting from life or portraiture.

Unlike the simple, utilitarian quality of Gormley's workshop spaces, Tom Philips' studio is more an emphatic work of architecture. Within the tower, the main stair to the first floor wraps around a column finished in a yew veneer, which contains a series of niches and shelves to hold Philips' collection of books and objects. From the first-floor reading area and the main studio level, a beautiful steel stair rises up to the mezzanine. Its form alludes to the spiral staircase in the Musée Gustave Moreau, a museum dedicated to the eminent Symbolist painter in Paris. The way in which the stair delicately unravels may be thought of as the "blossoming" or unfolding outward and upward of the interior of the tower towards the roof and the sky.

The stair is a combination of a straight and a spiral flight, which gave rise to an extremely complex profile for the inner stringer. Because of this complexity, working drawings for the staircase were quite rudimentary, with considerable responsibility placed on the steelwork fabricator. Both treads and stringers are cut from flat, mild-steel plate terminating at mezzanine level on a channel edge profile. Typical details were not able to describe the precise curve of the inner stringer and no setting-out dimensions were given. Instead, the start and finish points of the staircase were marked on-site and the steelwork fabricators took their own dimensions in order to construct the stair.

The spiral portion of the stair was fabricated around a mild-steel circular hollow section of 8mm (⁵⁄₁₆in) thickness. This was then flame-cut to the architect's site-marked curve. To avoid distortion, the steel was cut in short runs with a break to allow the metal to cool between cuts. Treads were made from 6mm (¼in) thick mild-steel plate welded onto a 25 x 25mm (1 x 1in) mild-steel angle. The quality of the welding is highly impressive, with the length of weld and the centres between them identical for each tread.

Constructed from thin mild-steel flat sections, balustrade framing is minimal. Paired vertical supports provide a connection between the flank of the straight flight of the steel stair and the main stair below. A panel of toughened glass preserves visual continuity between the two stairs and acts as a safety measure. The whole is finished with four coats of red oxide primer, which gives it a robust industrial feel, despite its sinuous elegance.

above *The staircase winds around a central column, finished in yew veneer, which contains niches and shelves.*

right *Meticulously detailed, the tough industrial quality of the staircase is enhanced by its red oxide coating. A glass panel prevents falls and preserves visual continuity between floors.*

Barcelona's ambitious programme of new sports facilities and urban infrastructure for the 1992 Olympic Games was an important catalyst in the city's regeneration. A new residential district was built along the seafront at Nova Icària; this originally housed the Olympic Village but now forms an integrated part of the city. The Olympic Village provided Nova Icària not just with decent housing, but with a whole new infrastructure. One

BACH & MORA
TELECOMMUNICATIONS BUILDING, BARCELONA, 1992

element of the thorough reorganization was a new local telephone exchange designed in 1992 by local architects Jaume Bach and Gabriel Mora. The building is in two parts, set on opposite sides of a street at a junction. The side that contains offices and workshops is housed in a sleek elliptical tower with slit windows set into ribbed aluminium cladding.

On the opposite side of the street, a prismatic, rectangular block containing technical installations leans towards the curved tower. This block is clad in grey stone, with small square windows punched into its smooth surface. The two parts are united by a wedge-shaped bridge which supports a telecommunications mast, boldly indicating the building's function. The dynamic composition of bridge and mast is a homage to both Russian Constructivism and the intentions of the master plan, which envisaged that major elements of Nova Icària would be bound together by bridges at main intersections. In some ways, the technical block resembles a sculpture, with no contents other than form itself – Bach and Mora are part of a current generation of Barcelona architects who relish such dramatic effects of abstraction and neutrality.

Yet although the technical building is essentially a hermetically sealed block, its monolithic mass is animated by a tall window cut into the main street elevation, revealing part of the main stair. The stone external wall is slightly inclined, so that the lowermost flight of stairs projects beyond the wall line, creating a striking stepped form, which casts changing geometric patterns of shadow. The line of the glazing follows the notches of the stair, stepping down the wall. The cleanly minimal stair is simply constructed from concrete faced with slabs of stone 30mm (1¼in) thick. A solid concrete balustrade is plastered, painted and topped with a crisply detailed handrail made of 3mm (⅛in) thick stainless-steel tube. Set in its "shop window", the stair forms a slightly theatrical spectacle from the street, drawing attention to Bach and Mora's elegant and unusual design solution.

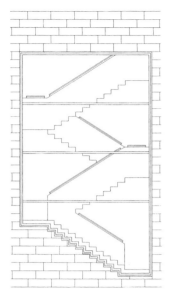

Elevation of staircase

left *A great glazed opening like a store window displays the staircase to striking effect. The lowermost flight of steps projects beyond the wall line.*

below *The staircase forms a theatrical element in the block containing technical installations. This is linked by a bridge to a curved office tower.*

One of the most enticing aspects of the few remaining traditional houses in Osaka or Kyoto is the way in which they manage to provide a variety of spatial experiences on one site. The narrow street frontages lead to a maze of rooms and small courts, each with character and a strong sense of place. Japanese architect Tadao Ando captures some of the traditional complexity of urban spaces in his Galleria Akka in Osaka's Minaki district.

TADAO ANDO
GALLERIA AKKA, OSAKA, 1990

above With Ando's characteristic precision and elegance, stairs and walls are executed in concrete poured in situ.

Set against contemporary urban conditions of sensory chaos, visual saturation and transient pleasures, Ando's architectural work embraces a contemplative, ascetic realm of stillness and abstraction. Monastic in their rigour and plainness, his buildings embody a rare mastery of light and materials that seeks to reconnect mankind with nature. Throughout his career, Ando has consistently asserted that architecture must be more than an autonomous art form and must strive to enrich the human spirit. Yet the lucidity of such a proposition belies the complex interaction of concepts and concerns that underscores the superficial simplicity of his buildings.

Essentially self-taught in architecture, Ando has learned to sense and experience space intuitively, rather than through conventional academic theory and practice. Despite exposure to many different sorts of buildings on his travels, the most powerful influence on Ando's work remains the traditional architecture of his own country. Yet the outcome of this influence is not any slavish recreation of vernacular forms and styles. Instead, Ando reinterprets the immemorial, elemental aspects of traditional Japanese architecture such as the effects of light and minimal materiality.

To his austere buildings, Ando brings a spirit of place that explores and responds to the individual qualities and regional vernacular of each site, thereby rooting his work in both the universal and the particular. In Galleria Akka, he has added a third dimension and, rather than making an elaborate jigsaw pattern of open spaces defined by single-storey rooms, he creates something that in its intricacy resembles a Japanese wooden puzzle in which the small pieces are fitted together with extreme ingenuity to make a sphere or cube. Set in a chaotic array of low-rise commercial buildings, Galleria Akka is a rectilinear space on a

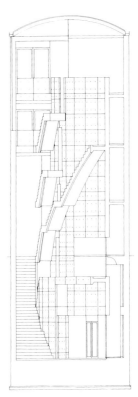

Section through the gallery

right Illuminated by a series of floor lights, the stairs wind and weave their way up through the imposing central atrium, giving access to the stores and art galleries on all floors.

above *A barrel-vaulted glass roof brings light down into the canyon-like slit of the central atrium.*

left *The concrete walls have a luminous sheen of lacquer that dematerializes their mass and gives them a potent elemental quality.*

rectangular plot with a frontage of 8m (26ft) and a depth of 40m (131ft). The tranquillity of the building's exterior belies the drama within. A central atrium rises five floors from the basement, accounting for half of the building's volume. Facing it is a curved wall with a 28m (92ft) radius. Flights of ascending and descending steps pass each other on opposite sides of the wall, creating a three-dimensional labyrinth that gives access to the stores and finally to the two gallery spaces on the top floor. A translucent glass roof diffuses light throughout this cavernous and imposing space.

Ando's design exemplifies the way in which Japanese architects are ingenious at making a virtue of necessity. Although the compositional framework is simple and austere, the maze of circulation paths in the Galleria – comprising stairs, landings, ramps and balconies – helps to create a complex, almost theatrical spatial experience. Here the staircase acts as an unfolding promenade, weaving and curving through the central void.

Epitomizing Ando's characteristically austere use of materials, the stairs and walls are made of *in situ* poured concrete. Considerable care has been taken to ensure that these elements are as perfect as manufacturing techniques allow. The formula of Ando's concrete is a surprisingly standard specification, with the emphasis placed on the supervision and technical capabilities of the construction team. In fact, while the solid surfaces are of a remarkably high standard of finish, they are not without blemishes, often bearing the traces of successive pours. Just as the *raku* potter relies on the unpredictable nature of the kiln to create serendipitous designs and textures, Ando relishes the unexpected flaws and changes in character that can result from the pour. But he also regards the material itself as an essentially ordinary substance formed, moulded and finished by the manual skill of building workers. Immaculately crafted and lacquered with a protective coating, the concrete walls and stair have a luminous sheen and a strangely elemental delicacy that contradicts their robustness. When animated by changing light from the barrel vault above, the material assumes the compelling potency of mass transformed by nature.

The cast-concrete treads and risers of the stair are clad in thin slabs of black granite, chosen for its hardness and elegance. A simple balustrade made from gridded steel mesh encloses the exposed side of the staircase and landings. Small spotlights, protected by 10mm (⅜in) thick panels of safety glass, are set at intervals on the edges of the treads and along the landings. Resembling the lights on a runway, these dramatically illuminate the form of the stair as it soars through space, embodying the elaborate, perplexing dynamism of one of Escher's famous illusionistic drawings.

During the early 1990s, fuelled by a buoyant economy and the developmental catalyst of the 1992 Barcelona Olympics, Spain embarked on an ambitious public building programme. This encompassed a range of infrastructure projects across the country, such as the creation of new urban parks and squares and improvements to transport and communications links. Making good the neglect of the past – especially in the hitherto

GUILLERMO VAZQUEZ CONSUEGRA
TELECOMMUNICATIONS TOWER, CADIZ, 1993

underdeveloped southern region of Andalusia – and then swept along by an orchestrated crescendo of enthusiasm, people of quite different persuasions and professions collaborated imaginatively to exploit every opportunity they could create. The practical consequences of this transformation, as well as improved transport and communications, were a batch of impressive new public buildings.

To meet the growing demands of an expanding telecommunications network, new telecommunications centres were constructed in many major cities. In Cadiz in southern Spain, Guillermo Vázquez Consuegra was commissioned to design a new telecommunications centre on a prominent seafront site. This joins similar buildings by Norman Foster and Santiago Calatrava in Barcelona, symbolically signalling a new era in technological development that mirrors Spain's urge to dispel the ghosts of its past and prove itself a modern and advanced society. Paradoxically, the Spanish construction industry is one of Europe's least technically sophisticated. Buildings are still hand-crafted in traditional materials; much of their appeal lies in the frisson between this and the pared-down forms that in turn are often abstracted from tradition.

Part urban landmark, part technical installation, Vázquez Consuegra's new building consists of two elements: an office block that closes a gap on the Paseo Maritimo and a 114m (374ft) high telecommunications tower that soars up above the seafront. The challenge was to transform an essentially functional facility housing little more than offices and technical equipment into a building with a degree of civic presence. Vázquez Consuegra achieves this through a quietly understated form-making and subtle use of materials that owe a clear allegiance to the current school of elegant European minimalism, reflected and distilled in a Spanish context. Although perhaps better known for his work in the perceptive restoration of historic architecture, Vázquez Consuegra instils those projects which have been newly built with an equally distinctive style and sensitivity.

The building is organized around a rectangular five-storey block of open-plan offices attached to a wedge-shaped volume at the

right *Spiralling through the atrium, the concrete staircase has a chiselled, muscular solidity. As on the base of the concrete telecommunications tower, the marks of its fabrication are visible.*

Elevation of the staircase

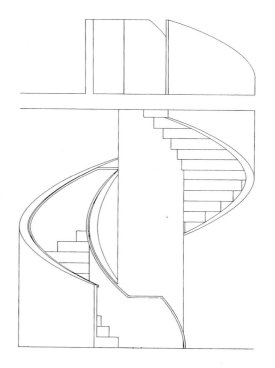

above *The staircase leads up to a landing cantilevered off the concrete shaft of the telecommunications tower. This leads into the tower and through to office areas beyond. A finely detailed steel balustrade forms a lightweight counterpoint to the massive concrete stair.*

left *Despite its solidity, the staircase has a crisply hewn refinement. A slender steel handrail runs around its outer edge. Treads and risers are made of timber fixed to timber battens.*

rear. From this wedge, the concrete shaft of the communications tower soars upward to an operations and viewing platform topped by bristling antennae. The base of the tower is enclosed to form a three-storey atrium around the building entrance. Marking the boundary between the public and the corporate realms, the atrium is a pivotal space which is endowed with an appropriate sense of dignity and drama. Light percolates down from rows of circular rooflights and through a tall glazed wall that separates the building entrance from the foyer. Materials are selected with care; creamy stone, dark polished granite, clear glass and white-painted plaster are brought together to create an atmosphere of calm refinement.

Dominating the tall, luminous space is the massive cylindrical shaft of the communications tower, a heroically scaled and unavoidable presence. But rather than being simply a static element, the tower is brought into play as a part of the building's general circulation. A helical staircase winds up from the foyer to connect with a landing at first-floor level, which is attached to the tower structure. Cantilevered from the concrete shaft, the landing leads both into the tower itself and through to the main office block. The stair also spirals down to the lower-ground floor, encompassing two flights in total.

The stair snakes round a chunky central concrete shaft, like a microcosmic version of the huge tower structure. Reinforcing the visual connection between stair and tower, the stair is formed from *in situ* concrete. The balustrade is cast into two fluidly spiralling low walls that enclose the stair like two sections of thick ribbon. Although the form marks of the concrete are clearly visible, creating a grid pattern on its surface, the finish is astonishingly smooth, like the best Japanese concrete-work. The bareness of the concrete contrasts with the lustrous surfaces that predominate elsewhere around the foyer. Gleaming polished timber treads and risers rest on timber battens fixed to the stair's concrete structure. Thin brass edging strips along the lip of each tread provide increased resistance to daily wear and tear.

Around the landings, the solid concrete balustrade gives way to a lighter arrangement of sharply detailed steel railings. Flat steel uprights 40 x 6mm (1½ x ¼in) support four intermediate members of the same size and a handrail made from a slightly larger 60 x 6mm (2⅜ x ¼in) steel flat. The entire balustrade rests on a steel angle (100 x 100 x 10mm [4 x 4 x ⅜in]), which crisply defines the edge of the landing. Fixed to the inner face of the concrete balustrade wall, the steel handrail extends down the spiral stair. The lightness and delicacy of the stainless-steel balustrade acts as a counterpoint to the weighty concrete stair structure, epitomizing Guillermo Vázquez Consuegra's finely judged approach to materials and detailing.

The present form of London's Royal Academy of Arts is the outcome of various extensions and remodellings, which have taken place over centuries and are not all entirely sympathetic or practical. Foster & Partners' refurbishment of the former Diploma Galleries, however, is a lucid contemporary addition that rationalizes the building's circulation and also restores and reveals its historic fabric. Named after American benefactors Arthur and

FOSTER & PARTNERS
SACKLER GALLERIES, LONDON, 1991

Jill Sackler, the galleries are housed in the top-floor space formerly occupied by the Diploma Galleries. These originally comprised a suite of three rooms with differing floor levels and heavy ceilings and cornices moulded around central rooflights. Such an arrangement resulted in uneven illumination and fluctuating temperatures, which were both unpleasant for visitors and unacceptable to lenders. Access to the gallery, via a rickety elevator or a stair wrapped around it, was also far from ideal. There was no separate

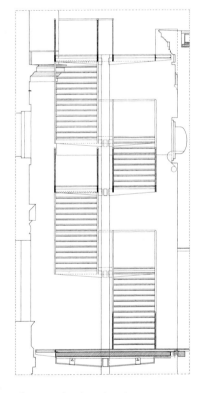

Cross section through staircase

entrance foyer and, since the only space for reception and ticket collection was in one of the galleries, visitor congestion was commonplace. Norman Foster (himself a Royal Academician) was initially commissioned to rectify the environmental conditions, but he recommended that all the problems be resolved together, while generally improving circulation throughout the building. All this became possible through the Sacklers' philanthropy.

When Sydney Smirke built the Royal Academy's Exhibition Galleries behind Burlington House in 1872–4, a narrow open slot was left to admit light into the rear windows of the older building. Over the years, these lightwells were filled with extensions and the rear façade of Burlington House became increasingly neglected and congealed with dirt. Clearing out the insertions and roofing over the lightwells created convenient locations for the new lift and stairs that now connect the Sackler Galleries with the rest of the Royal Academy.

In the eastern lightwell, a glass-walled lift like a bubble undulates smoothly and silently up and down. Visitors are transported up from the gloomy depths to an elongated lobby outside the trio of renovated galleries. The lobby brims with bright milky light reflected off laminated white glass walls and creamy stone floors. In the western well, a steel and glass staircase winds up to

above *A slim tubular steel handrail supported by a clear glass balustrade follows the line of the steps below. Old and new parts are brought together in an expressive yet sympathetic dialogue.*

right *The transparent staircase is a beautifully minimalist exercise intended both to reduce its own presence and to maximize the light in the stairwell slot.*

above *Detail of the translucent glass treads held in place by supporting tray-frames that slot into the steel stringers, creating an impression of effortless elegance.*

left *Poised in space, the steel and glass stair has an ethereal lightness and weightlessness. Radial segments of attractively translucent glass form the semicircular landings.*

connect with the other end of the lobby. In characteristic Foster style, the stair is an exquisitely minimal exercise, intended to reduce its presence and exploit fully the amount of light available. Pulled clear of the surrounding walls and supported by a free-standing steel structure, the flights are linked by a series of semicircular half-landings. Detailing is understated yet immensely refined, creating an aura of effortless elegance. Treads are made of translucent glass sheets held in place by supporting tray-frames, which slot into steel stringers. Landings are also made of the same delicately opaque glass, cut into radial segments to fit the semicircular form. Each individual flight is braced by steel supports that transfer the load to the central steel columns. Large panels of clear toughened glass form the balustrade, enhancing the sense of lightness and spatial fluidity. A slim tubular steel handrail precisely follows the line and direction of the steps below.

Daylight percolates down through the stairwell, filtered through the greenish glass treads of the stair like sunbeams in water. Within the ravine-like space, the gallery visitor can inspect the newly cleaned façade of the old classical building. The restoration has allowed windows to the rear of Burlington House to be unblocked and reinstated. This has been undertaken selectively, according to the requirements of the rooms behind. Those that remain blocked up are expressed blind, to recapture as far as possible a sense of the original architecture.

The Sackler Galleries are characterized by the generously wide and open lobby provided by Foster at the upper level. The spatial transparency of the staircase and state-of-the-art lift emphasize the increased clarity of circulation and the innovative nature of the display systems that could be incorporated as a result of Foster's reworking of the space. The long parapet on the original south façade was turned into a sculpture ledge by the demolition of redundant infill. The linear presence of this ledge both links the lift well to the staircase and emphasizes this upper level point of arrival and assembly, in direct contrast to the manifestly dramatic verticality of the lift and stairwell.

Foster's entire composition is a *tour de force* of detailing and design in which, despite the very tight perspectives, the visitor rising up through the stairwell has no feeling of constriction – rather an impression of release, even adventure. There is no laboriousness or rhetoric in his architectural approach, simply a calm dignity in the deployment of space, light and materials. The thick-walled, stark white vaults of the new galleries evoke Mediterranean archetypes that are sensuous and primal, quite unlike the formal classicism that the Royal Academy reworks in various ways. Despite such ancient echoes, the galleries and lobby represent a strikingly contemporary addition to the labyrinth of Burlington House and so do the new means of vertical access, which are executed with great style and sensitivity in the regenerated lightwells in the heart of the old building.

Seville-based architect Guillermo Vázquez Consuegra has a strong interest in the historic architecture of Andalusia and has carried out various projects, including converting the San Telmo Palace into the seat of regional government, and restoring a Carthusian monastery to house the Andalusian Institute of Historical Heritage (see pages 90–1). This project involved converting a house into new premises for the Andalusian Institute of Architects.

GUILLERMO VAZQUEZ CONSUEGRA
ANDALUSIAN INSTITUTE OF ARCHITECTS, SEVILLE, 1989

left *The upper level of the staircase takes the form of a gently tapering flight made of laminated timber boards. Subtle manipulations of the stair geometry create small benches along the open edge.*

right *The lower level of the stair is more simply detailed, with timber treads and open risers enclosed by a blue-painted steel balustrade.*

Axonometric projection

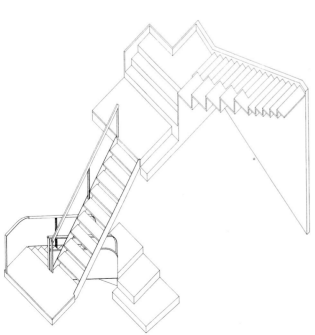

The refurbished building stands on the Plaza de Armas, the parade ground of the Alcazar, Seville's citadel fortress. In an arrangement that is characteristic of the typical Spanish patio house, it is planned around a central courtyard with windows facing inward.

The most extensive part of the refurbishment is concentrated on the second floor, extending the usable surface area, making alterations to the existing staircase and constructing a glass roof over the internal courtyard. The second floor not only contains the largest rooms in the building, but also incorporates one of the turrets on the citadel wall. This, together with the room between it and the courtyard, now houses the Institute's library.

A new staircase winds its way around the edge of the central courtyard. Changing in both plan form and materials as it rises, the stair has an intriguing, chameleon-like quality.

At the lower level it is a simple dog-leg with an intermediate landing. This part comprises a steel structure, painted blue, with timber treads and open risers. A solid ash handrail completes a minimal balustrade. By contrast, the upper level of the stair is rather more interesting, consisting of a tapering single flight, which is framed by a wall on one side but left open on the other. The stair is made of laminated timber boards so that it forms a continuous element and the boards have a polished, sensual feel.

Along the tapering open edge, the geometry is subtly altered to create a series of small seats, like benches in a Greek amphitheatre. In the absence of a balustrade, these offer some protection along the open edge. A straight ash handrail fixed to the wall unites the upper stair with the lower flight. Light cascades down the stairwell from the new glass roof that has been constructed over the internal courtyard.

High above the souk-like hustle and bustle of Neal's Yard in London's Covent Garden, Rick Mather Architects have carved out a breathtaking rooftop penthouse and tranquil haven from the shell of a former warehouse. Based in Camden, north London, the firm is renowned for the elegant modern design of its projects, which have included a series of restaurant interiors for the Zen chain and student housing at Keble College, Oxford.

RICK MATHER ARCHITECTS
COVENT GARDEN APARTMENT, LONDON, 1993

On entering the apartment, visitors arrive in a central lightwell, penetrated by an exquisitely minimal staircase. With dizzying nonchalance, sixteen solid maple treads with open risers cantilever out from the wall, but although they appear to project effortlessly outward, under the concealed end of each tread is a securing framework of clamping plates, fixing brackets, studs and fillets. The treads narrow as they climb, and the three lowest treads, with dimensions of 100cm (39in) wide, 45cm (17¾in) deep and 10cm (4in) high, are reinforced with extra plates.

Echoing the gravity-defying theme, a sliver of a steel balustrade, only 25mm (1in) in diameter, provides the merest hint of enclosure and support and, in keeping with the uncluttered, minimalist design, the stanchion arm returns to the wall independently of the treads. All exposed steelwork is shot-blasted and lacquered with a clear polyester powder coat for protection and a sleek finish.

Clustered around the stairwell is a group of cellular service spaces, including a womb-like utility room and a glacial orthogonal bathroom complete with sauna. As one ascends the sweeping vertiginous staircase, the compact hub of the lower level metamorphoses into an elongated loftlike space crowned by jagged sawtooth rooflights. The structural geometry of the existing shell forms a framework for Mather's fractured planes and insertions. The kitchen and study are defined by slinky white walls, while the rest of the living and dining areas collide in a sweeping open-plan volume. The sense of momentum is emphasized by the narrow strips of timber flooring streaking across the ground plane. In the very best tradition of the cannibalized urban loft, the architects have dexterously exploited the potential of a voluminous, unstructured interior to create a modern synthesis of space and light.

above *The stylish minimalism of the stairs sets the tone for this dynamically remodelled former warehouse. The upper section of the balustrade (just visible) acts as a protective railing around the balcony.*

above *Taking full advantage of the apartment's rooftop position, new glass skylights fitted into the existing framework of the building flood the stairway with light.*

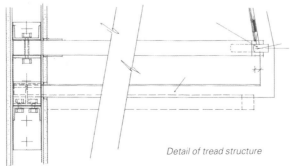

Detail of tread structure

85

In France, culture – especially as expressed through architecture – is a crucial aspect of national identity and pride. For centuries, French kings raised monuments to embody the power of the state, a tradition that was continued with unabated *élan* by the country's presidents

I. M. PEI
THE LOUVRE, PARIS, 1989

after World War II. Georges Pompidou famously commissioned the national arts centre in the Beaubourg district of Paris and his successor Giscard d'Estaing redeveloped the disused markets of Les Halles and transformed the old Orsay railway station into an art museum. Most recently, in the 1980s, François Mitterrand embarked on an enterprising series of *grands projets*, the most ambitious of which was the long-overdue redevelopment of the Louvre. Despite the magnificence of its collection, the museum desperately lacked modern amenities and was regularly overwhelmed by vast daily congregations of visitors. To revive its flagging reputation, it required radical surgery.

President Mitterrand appointed the Chinese-American architect I.M. Pei to oversee the controversial project. Pei is widely known as a Late Modernist, but his work eludes simple categorization. In the Modernist tradition he is devoted to rigorous geometry and the use of simple, often sculptural forms. But the key to his architecture is a willingness to examine a commission for what it has to offer, rather than impose a rigidly formal preoccupation. Pei looks at what exists and then considers what might be made of it, focusing on how people will experience the building as they pass through and around it. This enlightened approach, coupled with a reverence for high-quality materials and the way they are assembled, defines and unites Pei's body of work.

The Louvre commission was a comprehensive redevelopment, involving the reorganization of the museum's interior to incorporate the Richelieu wing on the Rue de Rivoli, recently vacated by the Ministry of Finance, as well as the creation of a new entrance to ease access to all parts of the building. In addition, a wide range of ancillary accommodation was asked for, from restaurants to underground parking. No site could have been more daunting and no programme more exacting.

Pei's strong geometric shapes form a contemporary counterpoint to the Louvre's elaborate "wedding cake"

above *Pei's staircase for the Louvre entrance hall is a classic open-welled spiral that celebrates his predilection for lucidly expressed geometry.*

right *Coiling languidly down from the main entrance, the staircase bears visitors into the great luminous hall. Risers are relatively shallow to ease descent.*

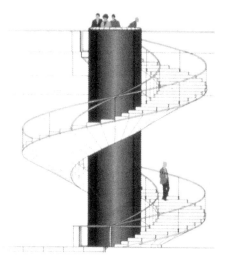

Elevation of the staircase

above *Pei elegantly resolves the automated aspect of vertical circulation by integrating a small elevator within the spiral staircase. Propelled by a hydraulic mechanism in its base, the cylindrical telescopic elevator rises smoothly through the open well of the stair.*

architecture. In a bold and deceptively simple move, he excavated the Louvre's central courtyard, the Cour Napoléon, as deep as possible, down to the water table some 9m (30ft) underground. In the middle, he inserted a gigantic square space, set at 45 degrees to the geometry of the surrounding courtyard. This is the Hall Napoléon, the new entrance to the entire museum complex, crowned by the famous glass pyramid, which acts both as a roof lantern and as a civic landmark. The centrally positioned subterranean hall facilitates access to the various wings of the museum and houses restaurants, bookshops and temporary exhibition spaces.

Visitors enter the pyramid from the Cour Napoléon, now redesigned as a civilized public square with fountains, pools, seating and bush-hammered granite paving. Once inside the great glass structure, they find themselves on a triangular projection of the ground plane which fills a quarter of the base of the pyramid. From this platform they descend a broad spiral staircase which coils down to the floor of the Hall Napoléon. Like a waterfall of human beings, visitors constantly cascade downward.

The stair takes its place as a key element in the cavernous space of the new Hall Napoléon. It affords visitors a clear view of the space as they ceremonially descend, allowing them to establish their bearings before commencing a tour of the galleries. Its generously proportioned treads and shallow risers of hard-wearing, cream-coloured Chassagne stone make it comfortable to use and combine elegance with durability. Toughened clear glass panels form the stair's gently curving balustrade, which is topped by a slim, tubular steel handrail. From a distance, the handrail appears to be floating in space as the lightness and transparency of the glass make the balustrade seem invisible.

Visitors can also enter the Hall Napoléon by a set of escalators or, perhaps more spectacularly, by a cylindrical telescopic elevator that rises smoothly through the hollow core of the spiral staircase. The mechanics of this contraption are exquisitely refined: an open platform rises up and down like a piston, powered by a hydraulic apparatus concealed in its base.

Like a finely crafted piece of jewellery, the staircase exemplifies the meticulous detailing and craftsmanship that characterize Pei's work at the Louvre, which throughout is distinguished by its lucidity, precision and elegance. The cast-concrete honeycomb ceiling of the Hall Napoléon, for example, has a sumptuous velvety precision, while the honey-coloured walls of smooth Magny stone are reminiscent of the existing historic buildings. Pei's work has dramatically yet respectfully reinvigorated one of France's most cherished national repositories of culture.

above *The hydraulic elevator in use. The underside of the staircase is clad in dark-grey steel panels, tapered to accommodate the curve of the structure.*

89

The fourteenth-century Carthusian monastery of Santa María de las Cuevas in Seville resembles a small walled city made up of a complex matrix of buildings. The monastery has an intriguing history. From here, Columbus prepared for his epic voyages, while after its secularization in 1835, it was transformed into a majolica factory by the British industrialist Charles Pickman. Furnaces and chimneys sprang up beside the towers and

GUILLERMO VAZQUEZ CONSUEGRA
ANDALUSIAN INSTITUTE OF HISTORICAL HERITAGE, SEVILLE, 1998

belfries. The outcome is a dense, chaotic and labyrinthine framework in which new elements have been superimposed over altered fragments of the original fabric.

In a challenging and ambitious programme, the Andalusian government has invested heavily in restoring the monastery and finding new uses for its sprawling collection of buildings. Local Seville architect Guillermo Vázquez Consuegra was commissioned to oversee the transformation of part of the monastery into the Andalusian Institute of Historical Heritage. Although the buildings that Vázquez Consuegra is converting are of no great architectural merit, thus giving him a relatively free hand, his response is as tactfully sensitive as it is confident. The institute's handsome new north-lit, concrete-vaulted workshop-studios are used for the renovation of historic paintings and sculpture – another instance of an apposite conjunction of architectural and cultural regeneration.

At the entrance to the institute is a large double-height foyer which leads through to various exhibition spaces. An elevated walkway runs around the edge of the foyer, leading to the institute's offices housed at first-floor level. Linking the walkway with the foyer is a symmetrically planned staircase consisting of a single flight of six steps rising to an intermediate landing. Two longer single flights are attached to this at right angles. Based on a simple geometry of intersecting slabs, the stair is made of raw *in situ* concrete. The two longer wings hang freely in space, supported by landings at each end. The deliberately processional plan has faint echoes of the great Baroque stairs, but materials and detailing assume an understated yet robustly functional quality appropriate to the setting.

left *The smaller flight is unprotected by a balustrade, so that the intermediate landing resembles a small stage.*

below *Treatment of the balustrade varies. One side of each stair is enclosed by a concrete wall, rendered a pale yellow and topped by a steel handrail; the other by three horizontal rails and a handrail supported by flat steel uprights.*

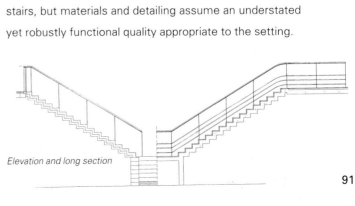

Elevation and long section

With their Georgian houses painted a riot of sugar-candy colours, the streets south of Notting Hill Gate in north-west London exude an air of studiously calculated bohemianism. Alan Power was commissioned to renovate a three-storey house for a couple without children; his brief was to open up the interior as much as possible and to create an inner realm as striking as the house's lime-green façade. The project presented an opportunity to

ALAN POWER
NOTTING HILL HOUSE, LONDON, 1999

above *Detail of the glass treads, supported by stainless-steel shoes bolted to a steel stringer concealed within the party wall.*

re-evaluate the way in which the house was organized and, in the remodelled scheme, the plan is radically altered. The raised-ground-floor entry level becomes the focus of the dwelling. Both the kitchen and the dining room were moved to this floor to create a sequence of informal, animated domestic spaces. A calm, luminous living room now occupies the first floor while the bedrooms are secreted on the lower-ground floor.

Such a substantial remodelling offered a chance to rethink the vertical circulation, in terms of both functional and dramatic potential. By eradicating the small, cellular rooms, the house has been transformed into a spacious volume. Topped by a full-length skylight, the stairwell runs along the party wall filtering natural light down through the three storeys. To fill the house with light and moderate the typical stacked horizontality of a London terraced house, Power decided to replace the existing dog-leg stair with a straight, laminated glass staircase enclosed by glass walls, which would connect the skylight with the new vertical space.

Linking the ground-floor dining and kitchen area with the living space at first-floor level, the new straight-flight stair, with its extensive use of glass, exploits the potential of laminating technology, structural silicone and newly developed, transparent structural tape. Glass treads and risers are supported by pairs of 48 x 70mm (1⅞ x 2¾in) stainless-steel shoes, bolted at one side to a steel stringer concealed within the party wall and on the other to the triple-laminated clear glass wall enclosing the stair. The wall rises up beyond first-floor level to form a protective transparent balustrade around the stairwell. Treads are made of 19mm (¾in) thick, clear toughened glass, edge-bonded to a bottom layer of 15mm (⅝in) acrylic sheet. The outside edge of the glass is dot-fritted – this creates a pattern of dots which diffuse the light, ensuring both grip and visibility. When back-lit by the low winter

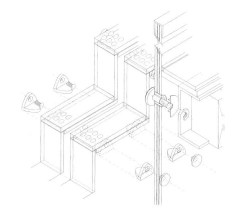

Detail of staircase assembly

right *A view of the underside of the staircase shows how light percolates down through the exquisitely minimal, transparent glass structure. The edges of the treads are dot-fritted for grip and visual safety.*

sun, the edges of the laminated glass glow blue-green and the fritting casts myriad shadows on the adjacent wall. The back edge of the glass and front edge of the acrylic sheet are stopped short to provide a rebate into which the 12mm (½in) toughened glass riser slots. The treads were bonded to the stainless-steel shoes with silicone "bubble tape".

The glass wall is a composite sandwich consisting of two sheets of 10mm (⅜in) thick toughened glass with an 8mm (⅝6in) acrylic layer bonded in between. Three 3.5m (11ft 6in) high panels are fused together with silicone sealant at the vertical joints. The wall rests on a channel set in the ground floor. At the first-floor level, it is bolted to an edge beam with stainless-steel pig-nosed bolts and extends 90cm (3ft) up beyond the floor level to form a balustrade. Each glass panel in the wall was installed as a single sheet bonded to the acrylic layer, which provides reinforcement and rigidity for lateral loading. The stainless-steel shoes were bolted to the glass with stainless-steel pig-nosed bolts; pre-drilled holes in the acrylic layer allowed the bolt heads to fit flush with it. The third layer of glass sheet was adhesive-fixed on site and the composite panels were bolted to the edge beam.

The strong vertical theme expressed in the staircase is continued in sections of laminated glass flooring at the head of the staircase at first-floor level and on the section of first floor over the front door. The staircase down to the basement is clad in limestone, with a sawtooth glass screen built into the limestone as a guard. The basement contains the relocated sleeping quarters, with most of the space given over to a master bedroom and a bathroom housed in a rear extension. The bathroom overlooks a low-walled patio, providing a bath with a view but also with privacy. Just as white-painted cupboards help to keep the ground and upper floors immaculately tidy, so a utility space that is tucked under the stair and the *en suite* dressing room helps maintain the pervading impression of spartan austerity.

In most Georgian houses, basements are dimly lit, but in this case, blue-tinged light floods down through the glass staircase from the skylight above. And, where a conventionally made staircase would have obstructed views and the flow of light, this delicate new stair imbues the whole house with lightness and transparency. The entire project is an imaginative fusion of contemporary construction technology and historic architectural fabric.

above *The luminous slot of the stairwell is incised into the house, bringing light down into its lower levels. The house is itself reorganized to create open-plan volumes instead of a series of cellular rooms.*

left *Toughened glass panels support one edge of the stair, thereby opening up the stairwell. Panels are joined together with silicone sealant at the vertical joints.*

95

Conceived as the "Pompidou Centre of the South", the Carré d'Art in Nîmes is a cultural facility without equal in the south of France. Encompassing a range of activities (library, art gallery, archives, offices and restaurant), it offers space for contemporary artistic creation as well as for reading, consulting, documentation and book-borrowing. The site lies in the very heart of the city, on a plot formerly occupied by a theatre that was destroyed by fire in

FOSTER & PARTNERS
CARRE D'ART CULTURAL CENTRE, NIMES, 1993

1952. From a limited competition held in the mid-1980s, Foster & Partners were selected as architects. Inserting any kind of modern building into delicate historical fabric requires astute sensitivity, but the challenge was compounded by the extreme antiquity of the Maison Carrée, the new building's immediate neighbour and one of the best preserved Roman temples in the world. So, from the outset, the project was underscored by a powerful yet invigorating tension between ancient and modern, which is clearly evident in the final built form. Foster's early sketches established his main preoccupations: to accommodate a large number of visitors in a focal space and to lead them through the building on a monumental "*scala regia*", or grand staircase. At the time, his buildings were still being categorized as High Tech, with all the inventiveness, informality and openness to change that such a label implied. The presence of the Maison Carrée encouraged him to relax his uncompromisingly forward-looking stance and engage with the past, increasing his architectural repertoire to include more traditional values of solidity and permanence.

Foster's new civic temple of culture is a cool, contemporary abstraction of its historic neighbour. Like the temple, it has blank side walls and an open front; like the temple, it is framed by a portico, in this case a generous, lightweight louvred canopy, to diffuse the harsh Mediterranean light. Instead of Corinthian columns, however, Foster's portico is supported on a series of extremely slender steel poles. The new façades are simple, refined and handsomely proportioned. The exposed structural frame of circular concrete columns is infilled with rectangular glass panels. Some are clear, some are milkily translucent like delicate Japanese *shoji* (rice-paper) screens.

The Carré d'Art is an iceberg of a building – five of its nine storeys lie below ground. On entering, dramatic views downward reveal the unsuspected importance of the subterranean. The building extends 20m (65ft) below ground, with the underground levels providing almost as

right *The monumental glass and steel staircase cascades like a waterfall through the central atrium space. Flights are supported on cranked steel spine beams.*

below *Translucent glass treads and open risers lend the heroically scaled staircase an impression of delicacy and ethereality.*

left *In a dizzying cacophony of steel and glass, flights of stairs weave vertiginously through the air. Minimal glass balustrades emphasize the structure's lightness.*

much space as those above ground. Protected by concrete walls, the lower floors not open to the public house a vast repository of books. From two levels below ground upward, floors are publicly accessible, lit by large funnels that transmit light from above.

The interior of the gallery clearly expresses another sort of tension, this time between solid and lightweight elements. This dialogue has underscored the project since it first emerged from the 1984 competition. As Foster always intended, the centre of the building is a courtyard rising full height to a gently pitched glazed roof. Below the roof a fabric membrane is stretched to generate a soft, even light. Various gallery, library and administration spaces are arranged around the internal courtyard. At the top of the building visitors can survey the grandeur of the 1700-year-old Maison Carrée from an open-air terrace restaurant that forms a delightful external room on the roof.

The major set-piece element is a monumental glass staircase that cascades down through the internal courtyard. This device has been used by Foster on other occasions, notably at the Sackler Galleries in London's Royal Academy of Arts (see pages 78–81). But the scale of the Sackler stair seems modest when compared to the heroic dimensions of the Carré d'Art, more appropriate to a film set from a Busby Berkeley musical. Proclaiming vertical movement as the building's dominant element, the huge focal staircase structures one's encounters with the various spaces and levels of the building and frames changing views of the townscape outside. It also forms part of a strategy for transmitting natural light down into the lower levels of the building. Daylight filters through translucent treads made of thin sheets of sandblasted glass. Risers are left open, adding to the permeability and lightness of the whole structure. Like a great waterfall of glass gushing through the building, the staircase sparkles as light reflects off and through its gleaming surfaces. At lower levels, where the library is located, filtered daylight transforms what would otherwise have been a gloomy pit into an exhilarating grotto.

Cross section through central courtyard

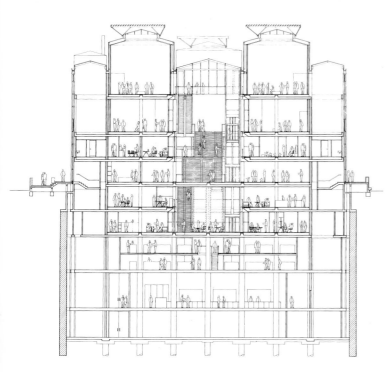

The glass treads are each held in place by steel frames and by brackets bolted to steel stringers. However, the main structural load is taken by cranked box beams that run down the spine of each flight. Springing out from the structural spine, the glass treads appear weightless, simply floating in mid-air. The structure is painted white to reinforce this pervading sense of lightness and ethereality. Detailing of the balustrades displays characteristic finesse and fastidiousness on the part of Norman Foster. Self-supporting sheets of clear toughened glass are slotted into the steel stringer pieces. A simple tubular steel handrail, which seems to hover above the balustrade, completes the exquisitely minimal composition. Grappling with a complex programme on a constricted and highly sensitive site, Foster displays his customary mastery of both abstraction and neutrality throughout the Carré d'Art.

Pringle Brandon's new offices for intellectual property specialists BTG marked a decisive break with tradition for the large and inherently conservative company. BTG originally occupied an eight-floor office block, but gradually outgrew it and commissioned Brandon to provide a more flexible and informal working environment in an office development close to St Paul's Cathedral. Arranged over two floors, the design had to accommodate

PRINGLE BRANDON
BTG OFFICES, LONDON, 1997

open-plan working areas for 150 staff, plus a suite of fourteen rooms for business meetings, some individual offices for patent lawyers, a library and a staff café. The aim throughout the project was to increase internal interaction and communication, so the conventional cellular office arrangement was dispensed with. For a firm with orthodox corporate taste, the resulting new offices represent a bold move, involving a combination of strong colour, transparency and a fluid, open plan that is deliberately calculated to instigate new ways of working.

The tone of these new offices is set on arrival, as visitors are greeted by a huge, textured, green, curved wall leading to a circular reception space that is surrounded by etched-glass screens. Off this is a series of meeting rooms named after notable inventors, which leads through to a library space overlooking the staff café. Conceived as the social focus of the new offices, the café is an airy, double-height space animated by translucent glass screens and by bold, colourful furniture. Turquoise-upholstered bar stools cluster around a boat-shaped bar, that is itself sitting on an island of mosaic tiles.

The café's mezzanine level is reached by a single-flight staircase made of gleaming stainless steel and glass. In common with the other new elements, the staircase adopts an organically inspired architectural language of fluid, streamlined forms, inscribing an arc in plan as it gently curves upward to the mezzanine. Its curved, single-flight form is unorthodox, but the stair is intended to be a major set piece in the café space. The geometry of the stair follows the curve of an adjacent etched-glass screen wall.

A pair of curved steel stringers provides support for elegantly slim treads made of sheets of sandblasted translucent glass held in steel frames. The form of the balustrade is also unusual, with curved steel ribs supporting a tubular steel handrail and slender horizontal intermediate rails. The ribs bow out from the stringers like the hull of a great ship, or a ribcage, reinforcing the sinuous, organic theme of the interior.

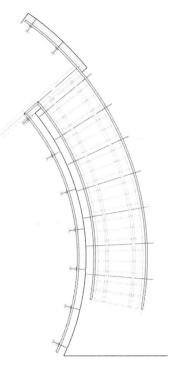

Plan of the staircase

right *Winding sinuously up to the mezzanine level, the staircase resembles a giant ribcage or a ship's hull. Spiky curved ribs support a tubular steel handrail.*

below *Treads are made of sheets of sandblasted glass held in steel frames.*

Utility has always been an important element of staircase design. Away from the seductive drama of glamorous entrance halls, boutiques and houses contain a multitude of more modest staircases often tucked out of sight playing basic but invaluable roles. Designed

UTILITY WORKS

for tight spaces and uncompromising settings, such stairs provide emergency escape routes or service access to roofs and basements. This generates a distinctive aesthetic of bold functionalism that strips form to its raw essentials and celebrates the tough, industrial qualities of materials such as concrete, steel and metal mesh.

Interest in the aesthetics of use and necessity started with the rise of Modernism at the beginning of the twentieth century, which sought to sweep away the excess and ornament of the previous age. Modernist architects were fascinated by industrial and marine structures and this was reflected in the design of elements such as staircases. Balustrades were copied from ships and the bare-boned simplicity of industrial access stairs often constituted as powerful an image as the ornate classicism of the late nineteenth century. Current strands of High Tech architecture are an extension of this obsession with industrial forms and processes, but this is becoming increasingly refined, despite its production-line origins. Yet, many architects still relish solving the problems of staircase design in ways that owe a clear debt to the robust legacy of industrial catwalks, gantries and spiral escape stairs.

Rows of staircases in the multi-purpose arena in Cologne by Architekturbüro Böhm generate a powerful rhythm that celebrates an aesthetic of bold functionalism.

Numerous community centres serve the socially deprived areas of New York City, but in the past there has been a tendency to make such buildings fortress-like and impregnable, protecting them against the very people they are trying to serve. Fear of vandalism and other acts of crime or mischief impact upon the architecture, giving rise to a succession of grim, institutional buildings. Although such issues cannot be ignored, there are ways

NYCHA DESIGN
COMMUNITY CENTRE, NEW YORK CITY, 1997

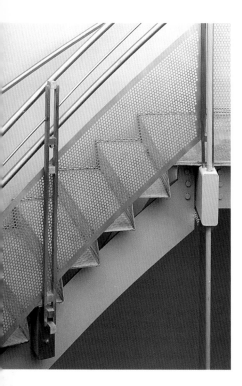

above *Both functional and durable, the staircase is stripped back to its essential structure. Treads and risers are made of folded galvanized steel plate.*

right *The stair and walkways spiral round the luminous rotunda. Mesh panels unify the various elements and discourage children from climbing the balustrade.*

to mitigate their effects, as demonstrated by this community centre in Brooklyn, designed by the in-house architecture department of the New York City Housing Authority. Founded in 1934, the authority is currently the largest public housing agency in the US.

The project involves the transformation of an abandoned courthouse in the Bedford-Stuyvesant area of Brooklyn into a new neighbourhood community centre. The scheme contains accommodation for a range of social programmes run by the Police Athletic League, aimed at local teenagers. Both daytime and evening activities are provided. The challenge of the brief was to adapt the former courthouse to house a new set of facilities and spaces. The solution involved recreating the original courthouse rotunda as the principal vertical element and introducing an additional level into the double-height courtroom on the first floor.

The four-storey-high rotunda, which had been filled in as part of a previous renovation during the 1950s, has now been reconstituted as the visual and programmatic link between the building's public entrance and the upper levels. It forms the key architectural element connecting the various new spaces, as well as acting as an informal social hub in its own right. Its rejuvenated role is emphasized by the choice of materials. Tough external materials that would not normally be associated with the inside of public institutions, such as slate and steel, reinforce the notion that the building is democratically accessible to everyone, thereby encouraging people to enter and to take advantage of the programmes that are on offer. Such inherently durable materials are also able

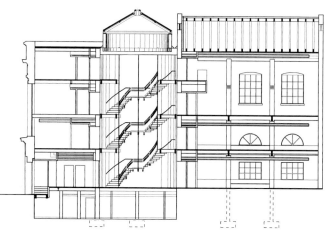

Cross section through the rotunda

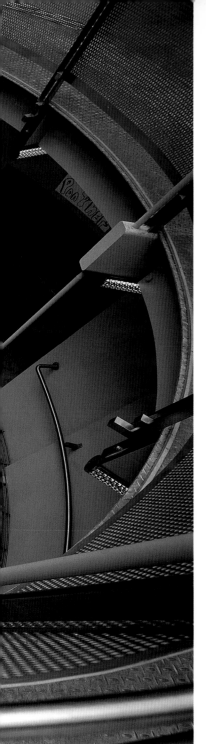

to withstand the hard wear that results from the constant traffic, and require a low level of maintenance.

Reincarnated as the fulcrum of the building, the rotunda is a tall, cylindrical volume that is bathed in the natural light that pours down through its glazed roof. A new staircase and walkway wind up through the space, connecting the building's various spaces and activities. The strong geometry of the rotunda dictated the configuration of the staircase. Each level of the stair consists of two flights of nine risers, joined together by an intermediate landing. Stair and landing occupy a third of the circumference of the rotunda, with the walkway occupying the remaining two thirds. In plan, each flight of stairs is based on a segment of 40 degrees, divided into eight gently tapering radial treads.

Designed to be both functional and durable, the stair is stripped down to its basic structure. Nothing is concealed; all parts are legibly and lucidly expressed. Treads and risers are made from thin folded sheets of galvanized diamond-steel plate. A series of steel beams approximately 1.5m (5ft) long provides the main means of structural support. Each beam spans radially between the existing masonry wall of the rotunda and vertical steel tension rods attached to the roof structure. The original

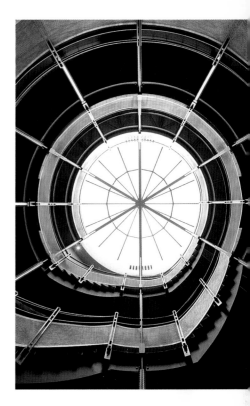

above *Reincarnated as the hub of the building, the rotunda is animated by natural light that enters through its glazed roof.*

above *All parts of the staircase structure are clearly expressed. A network of steel tension rods adds extra support and sustains the illusion that the stair is floating free of the walls of the rotunda.*

aim was to cantilever the beams off the walls, but owing to concerns over the strength of the existing masonry structure, a system of tension rods was introduced. A traditional post-and-beam system would have been easier to build, but the effect would have been to ground the stair, making the structure overly cumbersome. Instead, the network of thin steel tension rods sustains the illusion that the stair is somehow detached from the rotunda walls and simply floating in space.

The arrangement of the balustrade reflects a number of safety considerations. Vertical stainless-steel uprights support curved panels of perforated steel mesh, intended as much to discourage children from climbing the balustrade as to prevent them from falling. The mesh panels unify the stair and walkway and reinforce the project's robust, industrial quality. Concern was expressed by the client that the traditional level of handrail would be too low, so an extra rail was added at a height of 1.37m (4ft 6in). The handrail consists of three curved tubular steel rails supported by the vertical steel uprights. A single tubular steel handrail runs around the outer wall of the rotunda. Picking up on the radial rhythm of the stair and walkway, fluorescent lighting tubes, wrapped in steel mesh for protection, are suspended from the steel structure. Despite the explicitly functional nature of the community centre, the entire scheme has a simple dignity and rigour, based on materials honestly used and construction clearly expressed.

Zurich University is Switzerland's largest, occupying a district just to the east of Zurich city centre. The university's existing dental school building dates from the turn of the century and by the mid-1990s the school was in pressing need of more space. Theo Hotz was commissioned to design a new block housing treatment and training facilities. Slotted into a site adjacent to the main complex, the new three-storey building contains a dental

THEO HOTZ
DENTAL SCHOOL, ZURICH, 1996

left *Contained in a glass stair tower, the steel staircase has a lightness of form emphasized by open risers and fastidious detailing. Lateral stability is provided by cross-braced tensile cables attached underneath each flight.*

clinic on the first floor, with student laboratories and workshops above. A special dental clinic for elderly and disabled patients occupies the ground floor.

The new building is a crisply articulated prismatic volume, its clear glass walls strategically screened and shaded by an external layer of louvres that diffuse heat build-up and glare. The architectural language is modest, yet has a clean, geometric formalism. A glazed elevated walkway at first-floor level links the original building with the new extension. Tinted yellow foil set in panes of laminated toughened glass gives the bridge a striking, if curiously jaundiced, appearance. The bridge docks into a clear glass tower that has been pulled clear of the main building volume. Within this tower are a lift and a staircase, set on either side of a small lobby.

The 16m (52ft) high tower is supported by a steel beam and column grid tied back to the concrete floors of the new building. Double-glazed panels 2m (6ft 6in) high are hung on stainless-steel rods 30mm (1³⁄₁₆in) in diameter, which are suspended from the steel roof structure. All the steelwork is painted white, including the stringers that carry the staircase. Cross-braced tensile cables attached to the underside of each flight provide lateral stability.

above *Linked to a bridge that connects with the rest of the dental school, the crisp, prismatic glass stair tower is pulled clear of the new building volume.*

(The same cross-bracing is also employed on the walls of the glass bridge link.) Landings and treads are formed from sheet steel trays filled with mortar and finished with 2mm (³⁄₃₂in) black linoleum. As the stair is set almost flush with the external wall, the glazing acts as a balustrade on the stair's outside edge. A slender, stainless-steel tubular handrail is fixed to the steel rods that hold up the external glazing. On the stair's inside edge, the tower's steel structure supports the handrail and a balustrade of toughened glass panels etched with translucent horizontal bands. The entire composition is simple and robust, with structure and construction lucidly expressed.

Axonometric projection

109

Building mainly in his native Germany, Heinz Bienefeld combined in his architecture a modern constructional sensibility and the inherited wisdom of everyday craftsmanship. He worked on a modest scale, on a series of houses, schools and churches that allowed him to control all aspects of form and detail. For Bienefeld (who died in 1995), architecture was the realization of precisely constituted and carefully crafted construction. One of

HEINZ BIENEFELD
HAUS HEFENDEHL, KIERSPE, 1992

Bienefeld's many memorable domestic designs was for the Hefendehl House at Kierspe, located in the Ruhr Valley. The commission involved renovating and extending an existing one-storey house built in the early 1960s, a feature of which was a narrow covered walkway running along the main elevation, linking the house with a garage. In Bienefeld's remodelling, the walkway is transformed into a two-storey glass conservatory that acts as a winter garden – a luminous transitional space mediating between inside and outside.

The house has been reorganized with the living and kitchen spaces at ground level and the bedrooms on a new first floor. An elegant straight-flight staircase leads up through the winter garden to a long balcony that extends along the edge of the bedrooms. Stair and balcony display a crisp refinement of materials and detailing which demonstrates Bienefeld's preoccupation with construction.

Treads and risers are formed from a thin slab of *in situ* concrete. The concrete is very precisely and skilfully cast, with sharply defined edges and a smooth finish. The undersides of the treads are slightly curved, so that the steps appear to bulge, giving the entire composition a softer, sculptural quality. The geometry of the curve follows the line of the concrete balcony above. Three uprights made from flat steel sections are set along each edge of the staircase. These support a steel T-section which forms the handrail, and two intermediate steel tensile wires strung horizontally through the uprights. The handrail is welded to the uprights, to create an elegantly minimal connection.

Everything is beautifully spare and understated, from the raw concrete and the grey-painted steel to the exceedingly fine tensile wires. Colour is sporadically used to enliven the composition, but otherwise an industrial palette of greys prevails. Here, as with all his domestic projects, Bienefeld's attention to and mastery of detail is reflected throughout.

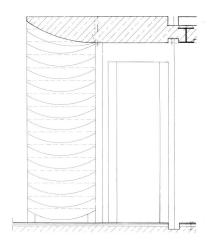

Cross section through balcony

right *The timber frames around the glass sliding doors to the internal spaces are painted a vivid blue and red, giving points of brilliant colour to the predominantly grey surroundings.*

Slotted into the shell of a former industrial building in the Marais district, Galerie Xippas adds to the vibrant life of Paris's contemporary art scene. Occupying three floors, the big, minimally articulated spaces form a neutral backdrop for the changing installations of contemporary art. The white-walled volumes have clean, uninterrupted surfaces, which conceal all services and technical equipment as well as other distracting signs of human

BARTHELEMY & GRINO
GALERIE XIPPAS, PARIS, 1990

left *Constructed out of black steel, the staircase reflects the tough spirit of functionalism that permeated the original industrial building. Its monochrome simplicity is emphasized by light-coloured surroundings.*

occupation such as doorknobs, handles and light switches. Only where the art is absent is this strategy adjusted, for example in a granite-faced lightwell at the heart of the building. Here the presence of architecture is signalled by rich materials adorning the otherwise plain surfaces. Colour and detail are thus used to achieve a very particular effect.

The spare materiality of the interiors almost seeks to deny the intervention of architects Philippe Barthélémy and Sylvia Grino, but their hand is evident in a series of beautifully detailed elements that evoke the simple yet curiously elegant functionalism of the original building. Among such details is a single-flight staircase that connects the gallery with the administration and staff areas in the building's basement. Composed entirely of black steel, its dark, sculptural simplicity is emphasized by the surrounding white walls. The stair sits in a narrow external stairwell, which is lined with smooth grey granite. The stone is so hard that it was possible to cut narrow slits in it for the stair's support points, which were then simply bolted to the concrete floor slab below.

Black steel stringers support slim open treads made of perforated steel. Angled steel stair supports are bolted to the stringers and, to conceal their appearance, the bolts have been capped with black plastic. The steel is varnished so that it gleams like Chinese lacquer. The detailing of the balustrade is particularly minimal: it has only four, very thin steel flats supporting an equally plain handrail. The elemental austerity of the stair forms an evocative contrast with the more florid period detailing present around the top of the stairwell.

Since the stair is only used by the gallery staff and is not accessible to the general public, conventional safety regulations could be waived, thus enabling the architects to explore a language of extreme refinement and lightness.

above *Detail of the staircase assembly at Galerie Xippas. The treads of perforated black steel rest on angled brackets, which are themselves supported by blade-like steel stringers.*

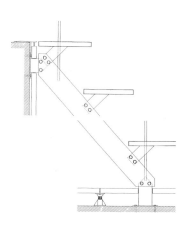

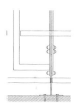

Typical details of staircase

113

In response to its dramatic expansion in the 1980s, Lloyd's of London commissioned Richard Rogers to design it a new headquarters. One of the main requirements of the brief was that the building should serve for fifty years, which meant that it had to be possible to update the various elements with a minimum of disruption to the main trading floor. Given the complexity of the brief, the design has maintained the clarity and directness of a

RICHARD ROGERS
LLOYD'S BUILDING, CITY OF LONDON, 1986

diagram and interprets literally the American Modernist Louis Kahn's concept of "served" and "servant" spaces. Rogers designed a doughnut-shaped plan in which a soaring, cathedral-like central atrium provides an unencumbered floor space for the underwriters' trading operations, while the stairs, escalators, service ducts and lavatory pods form six towers outside the main building envelope.

Making optimum use of an irregular site, the sculptural satellite towers create a strong visual and functional dialogue between these servant and served volumes. Mechanical services, lifts, lavatories, kitchens and fire-escape stairs sit loosely within the tower framework, easily accessible both for maintenance and replacement. Clad in stainless-steel panels, the towers consist of precast concrete columns, beams, landing and stair-slab elements, all of which are independent of the main frame.

While the dominant image of Lloyd's is that of a great sleek machine, the building makes use of fine materials such as stainless steel assembled with a craftsman's precision. In response to crowded site conditions, widespread use was also made of off-site prefabrication. One example is the composite stair and riser extrusion. The escape staircase treads are made from unusually large cellular extrusions, resembling a honeycomb, supported by a concrete base. As well as simplifying on-site installation, prefabrication has the advantage of economy of scale. All six escape stairs share the same structure and detailing. Perforated flat steel sections support panels of toughened clear glass and a simple tubular steel handrail.

A radical building for a conventional institution, the Lloyd's Building has become a familiar London landmark, with its gleaming steel-clad service and escape-stair towers dominating the labyrinth of streets below.

above *Inside an escape stair. Extensive use was made of prefabricated elements, which had great advantages on a congested site.*

right *Enclosed in gleaming stainless-steel containers, the escape-stair towers generate a distinctive profile above the medieval City.*

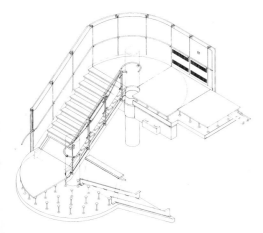

Cutaway axonometric projection

Studio BAAD's building for a textile manufacturer in the northern English city of Manchester confounds the stereotype of the glum industrial shed. Looking as if plucked straight from a sci-fi movie, it is a streamlined spacecraft-like construction clad in silver corrugated metal. Set in a dreary wasteland site, the building had to be secure, but this served to stimulate rather than inhibit architectural imagination. The shape is a potent deterrent to intruders: the

STUDIO BAAD
BEDMAKER OFFICES, MANCHESTER, 1993

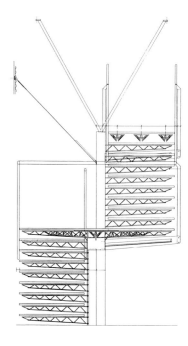

Cross section through staircase

curved walls are virtually unscalable, while wired steel outriggers on the vertical gables resist ladders. A shallow moat along the front elevation, crossed by a bridge leading to a glazed entrance hall, protects the metal cladding from vehicle assault by ram-raiders.

Since security dictated that the building had to be a hermetic volume without windows, it was important to provide an alternative visual stimulus. A continuous strip of glazing running longitudinally along the roof floods the interior with light, illuminating the first-floor showroom and diffusing light into the open-plan corridor and offices below. Oversized portholes punched into the exposed blockwork crosswalls between offices give lateral views through the workspaces.

The sleek silver carapace is penetrated at a single point, where the curved metal cladding gives way to a glazed wall enclosing the reception area. Within this double-height space, a massive, free-standing concrete slab rises to support the main staircase. The crude, almost hand-hewn texture of the concrete contrasts with the factory-made precision of the lightweight, metal-clad internal walls. Emerging from the slab is a glittering

right *Emerging from the concrete slab, chromed-wire brackets support stair treads finished in black rubber. The incisively detailed staircase explores contrasts in texture and materials.*

below *The staircase and entrance hall are both revealed by a glazed gap punctuating the steel tube.*

network of chromed-wire stair supports, each bearing a black stair tread finished in studded rubber. The cast-concrete spine provides support and acts as a screen, framing the route upward. The lack of visible fixings (the wire tread supports are glued into holes drilled in the concrete wall) is intended to suggest that the building's materials transform themselves as if by alchemy. Thus the concrete evolves into the chromed-wire supports, which in turn mutate into the rubber stair treads. The entire composition has a crisply engineered quality that explores the visual and textural contrast between different materials.

Studio BAAD has a reputation for designing compact, light industrial buildings on the tightest of budgets. This building exemplifies the worth of good design by creating a civilized working environment and raising the corporate profile. Yet it cost little more than the tatty tin-and-brick boxes that currently blight the inner-city landscape.

Herzog & de Meuron were asked to convert the imposing brick Küppersmühle building, a warehouse originally constructed in 1908–16, in Duisburg, Germany, into a gallery to house Hans Grothe's collection of postwar German art, an important assembly that includes works by Polke, Baselitz and Kiefer. The project has clear parallels with the architects' design for the new Tate Modern in London, but in the case of the Tate, only the external

HERZOG & DE MEURON
KUPPERSMÜHLE, DUISBURG, 1999

above *Sinuous and sensuous, the new stair winds upward to link the various gallery floors and create a leisurely promenade through the building.*

brick carapace of Gilbert Scott's power station has been preserved, whereas it was possible to incorporate most of the Küppersmühle's load-bearing structure into the building's renovation (although some floors were removed to accommodate the 5m [16ft] high exhibition spaces).

Three floors of galleries are linked by a new stair enclosed in a tower placed to the rear of the main warehouse block. The stark lines of the tower echo the Küppersmühle's muscular industrial functionalism. Narrow strips of vertical glazing are crisply incised into its terracotta-coloured concrete flanks. Inside, a sinuous stair winds up to the exhibition spaces, creating a logical and relaxed meander through the building. The warmth of the terracotta-coloured walls and the organic sensuousness of the stair give the confined space a remarkable, womblike quality. The proportions of the stair treads are intended to slow down progress slightly, so that visitors process through the building at a pace conducive to the heightened contemplation of art.

The galleries are calm and introspective, with simple white walls and cool stone floors. Daylight enters through carefully positioned glazed strips, evolved in an earlier project for Swiss artist Rémy Zaugg's studio in Mulhouse. The original windows in the part of the warehouse housing the galleries have been sealed up with scrupulously cleaned and repaired bricks of the same colour and texture as the original walls. This muting of the façade heightens the building's monolithic, elemental character and gives the new elements (such as the long window slits and an exquisite copper-clad door) a singular and surprising intensity.

Herzog and de Meuron's strategy of renewal seeks to respect both the building and its contents. The Grothe Collection has a handsome new home with all the amenities of a modern art museum and the Küppersmühle has acquired a dynamic new lease of life.

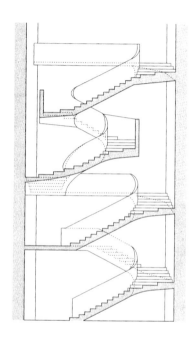

Long section through stairwell

right *Made of in situ concrete, with the marks of its fabrication still visible, the stair has a highly expressive organic quality. A slender steel handrail runs around its outer edge.*

The utilitarian nature of fire stations means that they are not generally architecturally compelling. However, architect Erkki Kairamo has explored concepts of speed, direction and movement to generate a striking fire station, which enlivens an uneventful suburban site in the Espoo district of Helsinki in Finland. Kairamo has used three elements – practice tower, fire engines and firefighters' poles – to animate and structure the architectural

ERKKI KAIRAMO
FIRE STATION, HELSINKI, 1991

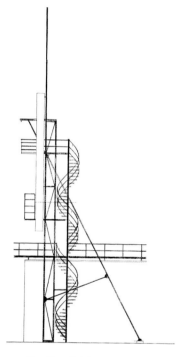

Elevation of stair tower

composition. The practice tower is placed on the north-east corner of the building for maximum visibility from the main road, the fire engines are stationed behind large, clear glass doors on the east elevation, and the fire-fighters' poles become focuses for circulation routes within the building.

The facilities are organized within a plain rectilinear box flanked by white planar walls, which is transformed by a robust industrial vocabulary of metal balconies, railings and spiral staircases. The practice tower might appear a slightly indulgent if highly skilful homage to Russian Constructivism, but its skeletal structure satisfies a very particular set of requirements. It acts as a training facility, the exact form of which was evolved in close consultation with the firefighters. Fragments of balconies, windows and stairs allow rescue exercises to be carried out by rope or ladder; the upper part houses a wind bag, a wind meter and radio antennae. Crowning the tower is the fire station number, a final artful accolade to El Lissitzky.

The tower's different levels are linked by a narrow spiral staircase, which is not for the faint-hearted. Wedge-shaped treads made of open steel mesh radiate around a slim central steel tube, reminiscent of a firefighter's pole. The balustrade is made of three horizontal steel tubes 22mm (⅞in) in diameter, supported at intervals by steel stanchions. The same steel mesh used for the treads also forms the landings.

The tower has a bold and even lyrical quality; elements are pared down to minimize the size of the structure, and the spiral stair has a surprising delicacy, once you come to terms with its vertigo-inducing openness. Such unexpected refinement makes it somewhat difficult to envisage teams of firefighters relentlessly pounding up and down its curved flights, but they do nonetheless.

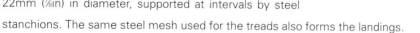

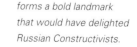

above *The skeletal tower forms a bold landmark that would have delighted Russian Constructivists.*

121

One of the problems of standard industrial sheds is that such buildings can often be difficult to alter if needs change or more space is required. This was the challenge facing Fritz Hack when he was commissioned to expand and reorganize a metalwork workshop in Tettnang in the south of Germany. Lying on the edge of the town, the site was a typical example of many industrial premises, cramped and disregarded, without sufficient room

FRITZ HACK
WORKSHOP, TETTNANG, 1991

for the introduction of major new elements. The two-storey building was a basic no-frills industrial shed and planning was further hampered by the need to allow for truck access.

Fritz Hack's solution to this unpromising and unglamorous commission is both inventive and pragmatic. Part of the storage area on the first floor has been converted to house the new offices and washroom facilities. Access to these new spaces is by means of a steel staircase contained within a glass stair tower that protrudes beyond the existing building line. Constructed entirely from glass blocks, the external wall of the stair tower defines a gentle curve along the edge of the workshop. The bulging wall also marks the new entrance to the building and its relatively unobtrusive form means that vehicles can easily negotiate around it. The use of glass blocks recalls Pierre Chareau's Maison de Verre in Paris, where industrial materials were transformed and elevated in the hands of the Modernist master. Here, the context may be more unassuming, but the block wall is a combination of both functional and aesthetic properties; a sleek, sensuous curve that diffuses daylight into the stairwell and the entrance hall beyond.

Within the stairwell a single straight-flight staircase leads up to the offices on the first floor. Despite its workaday setting, the stair explores a language of lightness and transparency that echoes the dominant theme established by the glass-block wall. Its apparent fragility is deceptive. The staircase is supported by a steel beam that runs down the centre of the stair like a spine. Crucial to the tight plan, this method of support helps to saves valuable space. The spinal beam is made from 12mm (½in) thick steel plate cut into a long serrated piece like the jagged edge of a saw. A series of circular holes 125mm (4¹⁵⁄₁₆in) in diameter is punched into the triangular spines, lightening the structure and creating a strong geometric rhythm of solid and void along its length. At the bottom of the stair, the beam is welded at right angles to a steel tube 76mm (3in) in diameter embedded

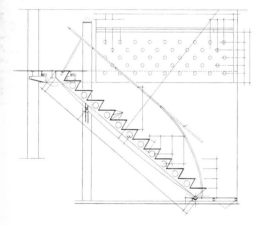

Long section through staircase

right *Treads and risers are formed from expanded steel mesh welded and shaped to form a strong, stable, basket-like structure. This is supported by the spinal steel beam.*

in a neoprene socket. The socket is cut into a bottom landing made of 3.5mm (⅛in) thick channelled steel plate, which is immensely durable and well suited to heavy use.

The spinal beam is supported at its top end by a short cantilevered member fabricated from steel flat sections. The cantilever is bolted to a steel column 193mm (7⅝in) in diameter which supports the upper landing (also made of 3.5mm [⅛in] thick steel plate). The steel column extends upward to form part of the balustrade around the landing. Treads and risers are made of expanded steel mesh bent and welded to create a structure resembling a metal basket that is light yet extremely strong and stable. The need for a more conventional means of support is thus avoided, saving room in a constricted space. Light filters through the gleaming steel mesh giving the tough stair a surprising delicacy. Forming a powerful yet attractive contrast with the basic industrial palette of silver, black and grey, the spinal beam is painted a bold red.

A simple minimal handrail made from stainless-steel tube 25mm (1in) in diameter flanks each side of the staircase. The handrail inscribes a straight line on one side, following the angle of the stair, and a graceful curve on the other side. Like fine ink lines sharpening and defining a drawing, these slender handrails add an incisive flourish to the composition. The balustrade around the landing is made of thin steel plate fixed to a 25mm (1in) diameter tubular steel frame. The balustrade is anchored by the extended column supporting the landing, its top clad in a conical tip of brass, which adds to the powerful vocabulary of simple geometric forms. Using the staircase could be a slightly disconcerting experience, as its lightness, ethereality and lack of balustrade all contribute to a sensation of walking on air. The expanded steel mesh treads might also pose a slight hazard to stiletto heels (but such footwear is unlikely to be standard issue in a metal workshop).

Hack's resourceful application of unassuming industrial materials such as steel mesh, steel plate and glass blocks is entirely fit for use in the context of a metal workshop, and extends an ongoing tradition of architectural invention that began with the Modernist exploration of construction and technology at the turn of the last century. Most recently this has been reflected in the evolution of High Tech architecture, a movement which has moved on from its early preoccupations with the arid logic of mass production wedded to extreme functionalism. The introduction of rationalized industrial processes into building construction to create neutral, flexible, expendable environments has today evolved into an increasingly diffuse and complex sensibility. Here, this relatively prosaic brief in Tettnang has been transmuted by Fritz Hack into an imaginative synthesis of texture, light and colour that animates and invigorates its surroundings.

In 1999, Glasgow staged the most ambitious celebration of architecture and design ever attempted in the UK, as part of the Arts Council's Arts 2000 initiative to make different areas of the arts accessible to a wide audience. Glasgow's aim was to bring architecture and design out of the professional ghetto with a wide range of events and exhibitions that would have a lasting impact on the city. The Lighthouse, Scotland's new Centre for Architecture and

PAGE & PARK
THE LIGHTHOUSE, GLASGOW, 1999

Design which takes its name from the turret-like water tower sprouting above a corner of the building, was at the heart of the programme. The centre, which is committed to presenting architecture and design in informative and challenging ways, houses two main galleries, a variety of smaller display areas, a 100-seat conference room and education and IT suites.

The Lighthouse occupies the imaginatively converted former offices of the *Glasgow Herald* newspaper, which were originally designed by Charles Rennie Mackintosh in 1895. The existing six-storey Art Nouveau structure now has an elegant contemporary extension by the local architects Page & Park.

As part of the building programme, the original octagonal water tower was renovated to accommodate a new staircase that leads from the third level to a top-floor viewing gallery. Conceived as a delicate, lightweight structure, the helical staircase appears to float within the massive red sandstone cylinder. The stair is suspended from the roof of the tower by four solid stainless-steel rods, 20mm (¾in) in diameter. The topmost rods are fixed to a beam structure in the tower roof, while the lower rods are screwed to support plates at each quarter-turn of the stair. The plates extend beyond the stair and are resin-anchored to the masonry walls.

A pair of 10mm (⅜in) thick steel-plate stringers form the helical curve. Triangular brackets welded to the stringers support wedge-shaped steel tread and riser plates. Oak treads, 30mm (1³⁄₁₆in) thick, rest on the tread plates. Each baluster is made from a 15 x 30mm (⅝ x 1³⁄₁₆in) steel section that is welded to the front edge of the upper tread and to the riser below it, passing through slots cut into the oak treads. Balusters support panels of 3mm (⅛in) thick perforated steel which form a curving mesh balustrade. A slim, tubular steel handrail snakes hypnotically up the stair, completing the composition.

above The lightweight helical staircase is suspended within the red sandstone cylinder of the stair tower.

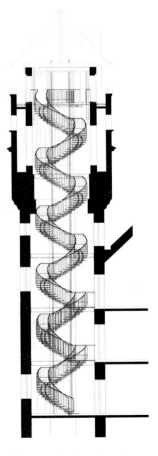

Cross section through stair tower

right The stair is suspended from the roof of the tower by a series of stainless-steel rods. Radial treads are made of oak and the curved balustrade is composed of steel mesh panels.

This apartment block in Cologne is slotted into a gap between two buildings, in the most unpromising of urban conditions. Barely 2.5m (8ft 2in) wide, the site is sandwiched between two unremarkable four-storey blocks which follow a conventional pattern of flats on the upper levels and stores on the ground floor. But local Cologne-based architects Brandlhuber & Kniess have risen to the challenge of making something of this inauspicious

BRANDLHUBER & KNIESS
EXTERNAL STAIRCASE, COLOGNE, 1997

above *Reminiscent of fire-escape stairs on a New York apartment block, the angular steel stair zigzags up the rear of the building.*

space. They have created an almost unbelievably long and thin building that nestles between the two existing blocks like a filling in a sandwich. Above the ground floor are two levels of tightly planned single-storey apartments, crowned by a duplex on the topmost floor. Crisply geometric glazing on the main street elevation signals the presence of the new building.

One of the challenges of the initial brief was to accommodate a store at the ground-floor level, which severely restricted the scope for vertical circulation to the apartments above. Brandlhuber & Kniess have addressed this dilemma intelligently and pragmatically by means of an external staircase that is positioned at the rear of the apartments. Occupants enter from the street and rise up one level internally through a narrow entrance hall, before gaining access to the external stair at the rear. This neatly resolves the problem of circulation and also provides additional security, as the external stair cannot be reached directly from the outside.

Constructed entirely of steel, the stair has a tough industrial quality that recalls traditional external fire-escape stairs on New York apartment blocks. Zigzagging up three storeys, it follows a simple dog-leg configuration. The stringers are composed of flat steel members which are 12m (39ft 4in) thick and 180mm (7⅛in) wide, laid on edge like blades. Rectangular steel plates 8m (26ft 3in) thick and 310mm (12¼in) wide are welded to the stringers to form the steps. Landings outside each apartment are formed from reinforced concrete slabs cantilevered out from the main structure and are topped by thin steel sheets. Intermediate landings consist of steel sheets welded to the stair structure. Flat steel uprights support both a tubular steel handrail and six tubular steel members that are smaller in diameter, which are strung horizontally to form a balustrade. Raw materials and simple welded connections give the entire composition an uncluttered honesty of expression.

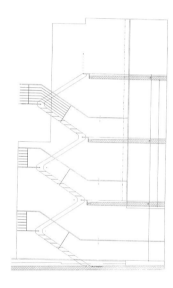

Long section through staircase

right *Raw materials and simple welded connections give the stair a lucid structural expression. Flat steel uprights support a horizontal steel balustrade and tubular handrail. The stair forms the main means of access to the apartments above the ground-floor shop, made necessary by the long thin plan of the building.*

Contemporary staircase design is distinguished by many aspects and its rich and unpredictable diversity forms the point of departure for the following, final chapter. From the macro- to the microcosmic scale, from monumental to domestic contexts, the staircase

MODERN ECLECTICISM

demonstrates its immense adaptability and pivotal importance in the creation of spatial and formal relationships. It continues to be a key element in buildings and powerfully representative of the various architectonic, symbolic and functional purposes it must serve.

Refined and reinterpreted by the major architectural movements of today, the staircase continues to evolve and diversify, its fertile history of eclecticism charged with a new and vital impetus. The staircase takes on many diverse guises – art object, structural idea, manifestation of pomp and manners, behavioural setting, political icon or poetic fancy. Circumscribed by the boundaries imposed by the human gait, the essential geometry of the staircase has changed more in response to aesthetic, architectural and cultural influences than from theoretical or empirical refinement. This has given rise to ever more diverse and surprising variations on basic formal themes. Allied to the skill of architects and designers are factors such as inventive exploitation of materials, advances in engineering, and increasingly discerning and demanding clients. Together, they form a launch pad for flights of imagination that dazzle the senses – stairs to seduce, stairs to astonish, stairs to beguile.

This dazzling spiral staircase at the University of East Anglia by Rick Mather is an example of the current diversity of design approaches.

Japanese architect Kiyoshi Kasai has created a house for his family that ingeniously exploits a cramped site. The main living area is contained in a single room 9m (29ft 6in) square and 5m (16ft 6in) high, linked by a short covered bridge to a separate building housing bedrooms. Except for sleeping, the family's activities take place within this single volume. It marks a radical departure from traditional Japanese houses, which are characterized by

KIYOSHI KASAI
FAMILY HOUSE, TOKYO, 1993

low ceilings and intricately partitioned rooms. However, there are similarities, particularly in the way the construction of the house is exposed. Interlocking diagonal timber braces are used to support the walls and diamond-shaped infill panels conceal extensive storage, leaving the living area pristinely uncluttered, apart from a handful of carefully chosen elements.

One of these is a long ramp that leads to the house's upper level. It connects through to a bridge linking the living and sleeping quarters. L-shaped in plan, the ramp represents an abstraction and refinement of the more conventional domestic staircase; it also elevates vertical circulation into an engaging and distinctly theatrical progress through the compact space. The ramp is composed of two parts. The main section is made from a single long piece of lightweight, woven stainless-steel mesh (not unlike a metal version of traditional Japanese tatami matting). Suspended from two rows of tensile steel rods bolted into the timber ceiling, the mesh ramp runs along one wall, rising gently to the upper level. A smaller ramp made from a thin sheet of steel joins the main ramp at right angles.

Suspending the main ramp frees up the space underneath and means that the tensile rods can be incorporated into the balustrade. The ramp strongly resembles a ship's gangway, and to reinforce its nautical appearance, the balustrade is made of lengths of chunky white rope looped through hooks and buckles fixed to the tensile rods and ramp. The resulting criss-cross pattern is unmistakably nautical and is playfully emphasized by a trio of porthole windows of different sizes punched into the adjacent wall. Kasai's witty appropriation of materials and his inventive use of space infuses the whole house with a robust informality.

Long section through ramp

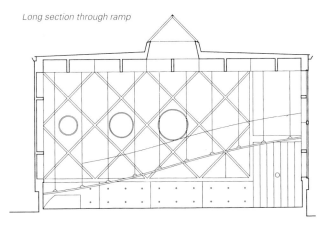

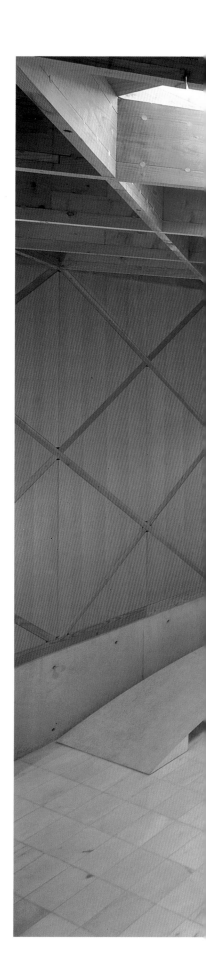

right *Suspended by slender steel tensile wires, the L-shaped metal ramp rises up along the edge of the living room like a ship's gangplank. Balustrades made of rope and porthole windows reinforce the nautical imagery.*

Since the early 1980s, the Miami-based firm of Arquitectonica has been earning a reputation for its flamboyant contributions to the city's skyline. Inspired by sources as diverse as Russian Constructivism and Miami's Art Deco tradition, principals Bernardo Fort-Brescia and Laurinda Spear have pursued a strand of witty, playful Post-Modernism that is both abstract and romantic. Whimsical elements and motifs often belie a

ARQUITECTONICA
ATLANTIS CONDOMINIUM, MIAMI, 1982

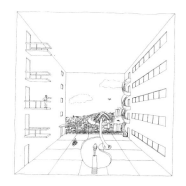

Cross section (top) and perspective of sky court

left *Set against a bright yellow wall, the chunky stucco spiral of the staircase winds around the central newel in a conventional manner, but its unorthodox setting has made it one of the most celebrated sights along Miami's waterfront.*

seriousness of purpose that only emerges on closer scrutiny. Using simple, childlike forms, surprising materials and vivid colour, Arquitectonica create complex architectural collages that exude an almost painterly quality (Laurinda Spear is also an artist) in their juxtaposition of flat surfaces and sculptural volumes. Dramatic and forceful, Arquitectonica's work is an ongoing exploration of the power of composition and contradiction.

The most photographed of all Arquitectonica's buildings is the Atlantis, a ninety-six-unit condominium apartment on Biscayne Bay south of downtown Miami, one of three such projects by the firm on the same street. More than any other, this building epitomizes the provocative, graphic quality of Arquitectonica's work. With its flat, blue-gridded walls punctured by an off-centre void, it has become an iconic landmark for Miami and has made modest inroads into popular culture: it was the setting for Brian de Palma's remake of the film *Scarface* and was immortalized in the opening sequence of *Miami Vice*.

The Atlantis is a sleek, narrow slab, eighteen storeys high, with a cube cut out of its centre to create a "sky court" or communal outdoor room for its residents. A yellow volume of identical proportions to the void lies at the foot of the building, as if just ejected from it; this houses a squash court and exercise room.

Set perpendicular to the waterfront, the building explores simple yet powerful imagery. On the south side, the glass wall is overlaid by a blue stucco grid, which acts as a *brise-soleil*. The grid is incised horizontally by cantilevered balconies, their linear balustrades like those of an ocean liner. Reinforcing the nautical imagery, the short east elevation facing the sea is curved, so that these lucky apartments have 180-degree views. On the north side, a

above *Boldly hanging over the north edge of the building, the deep-red stairs can be read at a distance, providing a compositional focus for the graphic façades.*

135

homogeneous grey glass wall is articulated by a quartet of yellow triangular balconies stacked above each other. On the roof, a huge red triangle houses mechanical plant and announces the building's presence to the city beyond.

Arquitectonica's particular brand of "PoMo" spiked with Art Deco and more than a dash of Hollywood could not be better suited to its Miami context of waterfront views, lush greenery and lavish lifestyles. With only six generously proportioned flats per floor, the Atlantis is very consciously at the luxury end of the market. Its most unorthodox feature is the elevated sky court, which offers even the most jaded condominium dweller a tantalizing frisson of danger and hedonism. Although it measures only 11m (36ft) square, the sky court appears larger because of its unexpected location in the building's curious off-centre void. Devoted to luxury and sensual indulgence, the court contains a hot tub and whirlpool bath, incongruously shaded by a towering palm tree. A curved yellow wall with a red balcony tactfully conceals the clutter of mechanical plant. With its breathtaking views and improbable palm tree, it is a surreal space.

For most residents, this compact slice of nirvana is accessed by elevator, but for the privileged few, a red spiral staircase runs up the south wall to connect the sky court directly with a handful of apartments. Intended more as a playful, sculptural element than a workaday stair, the four-storey spiral cantilevers out slightly over the north face, adding to an already vertiginous experience. The stair winds conventionally around a central newel and although its design may be unremarkable, its location is astounding. Painted a stimulating shade of red, its chunky stucco form can be easily read at a distance, a bold scarlet spiral set against a yellow wall, forming the compositional focus of the long elevations. Insouciantly poised in space, it is without doubt one of the most celebrated staircases in Miami.

above The sky court is a hedonistic oasis devoted to pampering and pleasure. The dramatic red staircase leads up to the individual apartments.

Like all brilliant ideas, the Atlantis building is distinguished by the searing clarity of both thought and execution. Fundamentally, the building is a pair of billboards sandwiched together, with a rather spectacular hole punched through them. Yet the juxtaposition of shimmering glass surface and cubic void is simply too seductive to ignore; it is as if you can see through a break in a mirror. With its mixture of wit and brashness, Atlantis is a quintessential Miami building, set plum on a blue-chip strip of city real estate with a view straight out of the movies. It is not so much a commentary on a lifestyle but a manifesto for one, in which power and privilege are taken for granted, even by its architects, who navigate these waters with accustomed ease.

above *The playful curvaceousness of the coiled red staircase contrasts with the rigid, orthogonal grid of the elevations. Colour animates and enlivens the massive apartment block.*

By the late 1980s the fortunes of the Century Paramount Hotel were languishing, despite its immense size and plum mid-town location in the heart of Broadway. In 1990, it underwent a facelift inspired by Philippe Starck, who radically transformed the interior. Working with his habitual brio, the French designer was encouraged by a particularly enlightened client, Ian Schrager, king of New York nightlife and creator of the legendary

PHILIPPE STARCK
PARAMOUNT HOTEL, NEW YORK CITY, 1990

above *Sweeping diagonally down across the Paramount's spacious lobby, the staircase is a monolithic, sculptural presence that is subverted by Starck's characteristic touches of wit.*

Studio 54 nightclub. Between them, Starck and Schrager have redefined the contemporary hotel as a place of cosmopolitan cachet and cool.

The revived Paramount opens up into a generously proportioned lobby that evokes the sleek, comfortable atmosphere of an ocean-going liner. Starck has spared nothing in his quest for stimulating effects. Small jewel-like lamps shed filtered light and furniture by Jasper Morrison and Marc Newson is arranged like surreal pieces on a giant chequerboard rug. The focal point of the lobby is a large canted staircase that sweeps down diagonally from one corner, linking the ground floor with restaurants, lounges and bars above. The scale of the stair is heroic, like a film set, and its tapering, irregular geometry reflects Starck's preoccupation with organic forms.

Nosing into the lobby like a big beached whale, the stair is conceived as a sculptural element in its own right. Clad in dusky grey stone to match the surrounding floor, it has a powerful monolithic quality, which is subverted by Starck's impish attention to detail. The staircase is flanked on one side by a curving wall, which is finished in gleaming, thin, burnished steel panels and is dramatically spotlit to cast scintillating reflections through the lobby. On the other side, frameless sheets of clear toughened glass set along the edge of the stair resemble a weightless, transparent blade. Tubular steel handrails inscribe a languidly wavy profile down the shining wall and glass balustrade, their sharply defined minimalism setting off the hulking mass of the staircase. At the Paramount and in successive hotel projects for Schrager, Starck's witty detailing and innate sense of theatre conspire to create a constant source of surprise and delight.

right *A clear glass balustrade runs like a transparent blade along the edge of the stair, forming a powerful contrast with the structure's massive solidity.*

Elevation of the staircase

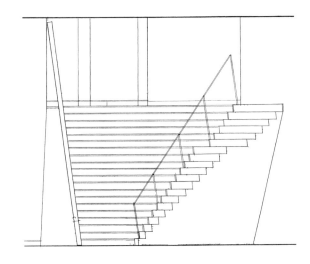

Steven Holl's new Museum of Contemporary Art in Helsinki seeks to redefine the art museum as institution, shifting away from the conventional image of the élitist treasure house to that of an inclusive public meeting place. A catholic collection, a wide range of events and extended opening hours are all intended to attract the widest possible audience. Located as it is in the centre of Finland's capital, Helsinki, within sight of the

STEVEN HOLL
KIASMA MUSEUM OF CONTEMPORARY ART, HELSINKI, 1998

left *Swirling gently through space, the staircase unfolds like a flower as it rises through the tall space. Black treads and white concrete structure impart a stark, clinical quality. The first-floor landing connects with a long curved ramp in the entrance hall.*

city's major sites and monuments, the museum is well situated to support the notion that art can act a medium for public interaction.

The building consists of an orthogonal block and a twisted curvilinear extrusion that houses the main set of gallery spaces. Between these two parts is a canyon-like void containing a long curved ramp that leads up to the circuit of galleries. Designed to make the most of the elusive quantity and quality of daylight available in this extreme northern latitude, the museum's curved section captures the warm light of a horizontal sun, which is diffused by carefully placed windows. Much of the daylight in the building – particularly in the galleries and the central void – is diffused by translucent glass. This both intensifies the weak Nordic light and imparts a sense of quiet abstraction and detachment from the life of the city outside. Progress through the museum becomes an introverted journey, yet release in the form of views out is provided by clear glazing at significant points.

Inside, asymmetry defines movement through a series of spatial sequences, so that the overall organization becomes transformed into a slightly warped gallery of rooms. These curved unfolding sequences provide elements of both mystery and surprise, which tend not to exist in a typical single- or double-loaded orthogonal arrangement of spaces. Instead, the visitor is confronted by a continuous unfolding of changing perspectives that expounds on the overall concept of intertwining, or "kiasma" (derived from the Greek letter *chi*, meaning a crossing or exchange). Unlike a hierarchically sequenced or ordered movement, this open-ended casual circulation serves to provoke moments of pause, of reflection and of discovery while exploring all that the museum has to offer.

Thus the underlying order of the Museum of Contemporary Art cannot be understood from a single vantage point but unfolds almost cinematically as the visitor moves through a landscape of interior space. Multiple lifts, stairs and ramps combine with split-level galleries to create many possible itineraries through the building, but the circulation always returns to the central void that is formed between the two intersecting

Cross section through museum

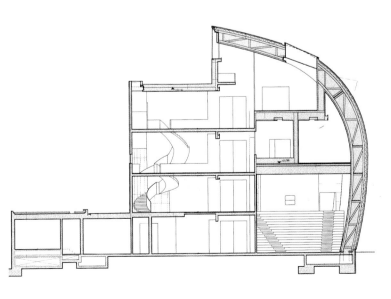

volumes. At the tapering end of this void lies an extraordinary curved staircase which functions as a key element of vertical circulation.

The staircase rises up through the entire building, but its complex and unusual plan changes from floor to floor. From ground to first floor it follows a conventional spiral, which then evolves into an ellipse for the upper two storeys. One half of the ellipse is a gently inclined ramp (from first to second floor) and the other half a curving flight of stairs (second to third). From third to fourth floor it changes again, into a straight ramp running along the edge of the stairwell. This mutable geometry generates ever-shifting and intriguing views, both from and around the stair.

Made principally of reinforced *in situ* concrete, the stair's sinuous, irregular form (it soon became known as the "pasta stair") required great skill and ingenuity in casting. Holl asked an experienced carpenter, whose task it was to build the formwork for the stair, whether the work was difficult. The reply was immediate: "It's not difficult, it's interesting." The faintly ribbed pattern of the formwork is still just visible, bearing witness to this process of construction.

Like the rest of the building, the stair is stripped to its anatomy, a compellingly stark, fleshless presence with the absolute minimum of adornment. The concrete structure is simply painted white, set off by black treads and risers. Contrast is also explored in the treatment of the balustrade. The inner balustrade is a solid concrete wall, which spirals upward like a thick coil of paper. The outer balustrade consists of fine steel mesh panels held in place by steel flats screwed into the edge of the concrete structure. Crisp tubular steel handrails run round

both sides of the stair, articulating and defining the sweep of its austere, sculptural form. Balletically poised in the tall stairwell, the stairs and ramps exude in their remarkable interplay a gymnastic power and grace.

Throughout, Kiasma is underpinned by the notion that architecture, art and culture are not separate disciplines but integral parts of the city and landscape. Through immense care in the development of details and materials, as exemplified by the swirling staircase, the new museum embodies a dynamic yet subtle spatial form, extending to the city on one side and the natural landscape on the other.

A fundamental task of contemporary art is to question values and issues that are usually taken for granted. From that perspective, Holl's museum may be considered particularly appropriate. It does not create a neutral background for art, but instead strongly participates in the questioning process, addressing conventional conceptions of museums and institutions and also the perception of art itself.

above *The supple curves and planes of the concrete stair structure merge into each other with an organic expressiveness.*

right *Supported by steel flat sections, a lightweight steel mesh balustrade runs along the stair's outer edge. The spiralling stair forms part of a network of vertical circulation elements that leads visitors on a circuit of discovery.*

The mews house in Holland Park, west London, that Pierre Botschi designed some twenty years ago for himself and his family contains one of the most remarkable domestic staircases in London. For some time, he had been fascinated by appropriating scaffolding systems in a pioneering High Tech spirit to create elements within the home. Flexible, economical and adaptable, the kit of scaffolding parts had many applications, but was

PIERRE BOTSCHI
MEWS HOUSE, LONDON, 1980

above *Open-plan levels are linked by the compact spiral stair made from a kit of tubular parts.*

especially suitable for staircases. Prior to this house, Botschi designed a spiral stair in his Kensington apartment that had no handrail or balustrade and consisted simply of treads supported by short lengths of proprietary scaffolding tube radiating around a central support. The treads were formed from small rubber-clad discs screwed to the scaffolding brackets. It was an admirably minimal, if somewhat precipitous solution.

For the larger mews house, Botschi applied the same design, but in this case the staircases spirals vertiginously through two revolutions linking the ground floor with the attic. To ascend is a daunting experience, not recommended for the elderly, the heavily laden or those with an aversion to heights, while to descend is an act of sheer faith. Yet Botschi maintains that his family quickly grew accustomed to the absence of handrails and the small circular treads.

Architecturally, the stair makes good sense. With so little floor space – the ground plan measures a mere 6 x 6.4m (19ft 6in x 21ft) – no garden and no view in any direction, the house was bound to be introspective. Reconfigured, its main appeal lies in the relationship between the open-plan floors and the staircase dramatically corkscrewing between them. Bedrooms are placed at ground-floor level on either side of the bathroom core, with the kitchen, dining and living space on the first floor. Above is a roof terrace cut out of the roof pitch, which is flanked by a pair of small gallery spaces.

As found, the house was in advanced state of dilapidation. Botschi rebuilt the front elevation in plum-coloured brick, placing circular windows on either side of a two-storey glazed arch. At ground level, the central panel of the arch serves as the front door. But the key to his remodelling is undoubtedly the winding treadmill of the staircase with its stepping stones in space, ascending boldly through the air.

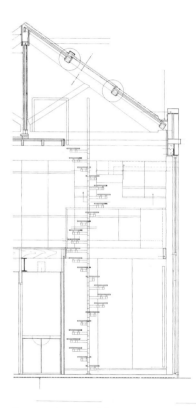

Cross section through house

right *The winding, gyrating staircase is a simple combination of scaffolding tubes and rubber disc treads. Its compact form and lack of balustrade are not for the faint-hearted, but it is an undeniably inventive solution to the house's lack of space.*

Designed by Madrid-based architect Rafael Moneo, San Sebastián's new Kursaal concert hall and conference centre occupies a prominent site on the Spanish city's seafront. The building is the outcome of a competition held in 1990, a year before that for the spectacular Guggenheim Museum along the coast in Bilbao. The name Kursaal (casino) is the legacy of a previous San Sebastián institution, an entertainment pavilion dating from

RAFAEL MONEO
KURSAAL AUDITORIUM, SAN SEBASTIAN, 1999

left *One of the flights of stairs that forms part of a dizzying network of open staircases and walkways sweeping visitors up to the various levels of the concert hall. The concrete stair structure is clad in smooth, honey-coloured stone, reflecting Moneo's characteristically refined approach to both details and materials.*

below *Imbued with a supple grace, the stair springs balletically from level to level. Translucent glass walls fill the foyer with a softly radiant light.*

the late nineteenth century. This new Kursaal revives the *belle-époque* tradition of large seaside buildings, and, like the Guggenheim, aims to become an icon for its city.

The key elements of the scheme are an auditorium and a concert hall, conceived as autonomous volumes clad in a homogeneous, translucent skin of laminated glass. Outside, the glass surface provides protection from the sea winds, transforming the volumes into a delicately diaphanous mass by day; after dark, the glazed forms function as beacons on a grand scale, electrified and elegant. Inside, the translucent skin moderates light into the foyers around the auditoria, creating neutral, softly luminous spaces.

Around the main volume of the concert hall, a free-form family of open stairways and viewing platforms weaves vertiginously up to the various levels. These generous promenading spaces for both seeing and being seen also echo the *belle-époque* model, recalling the lavish foyers and staircases of nineteenth-century theatres and opera houses. Moneo's contemporary reinterpretation employs a carefully chosen palette of materials and refined detailing to evoke an aura of formality and opulence. A network of staircases all conforming to the same generic design soar and fly through the tall volume of the foyer. In some places they seem to defy gravity, leaping across chasms of space, supported lightly between landings.

Proportions vary according to the expected flow of people, with wide flights at lower levels giving way to narrower flights on the upper floors. Treads and risers are clad in thin slabs of honey-coloured stone, concealing a concrete structure below. Durable and able to age gracefully even with intense use, stone was a rational choice, yet it also ensures an understated elegance. Balustrades are made from timber panels, echoing the horizontal timber-strip cladding to the auditorium volume. A seductively grippable handrail of light oak is supported on short steel uprights fixed to the top of the balustrade. Imbued with a sense of the dramatic potential of space and circulation, Moneo's Kursaal fluidly integrates the comings and goings of its diverse users.

The SGB advertising agency occupies the top floor of a turn-of-the-century grain warehouse at the foot of Telegraph Hill on the edge of San Francisco's financial district. Remodelled by Richard Fernau and Laura Hartman, the building now contains enclosed offices, workstations and the usual ancillary facilities for more than seventy staff. Fernau & Hartman's scheme began with the elegant, empty shell of the warehouse. Measuring

FERNAU & HARTMAN
SGB OFFICE, SAN FRANCISCO, 1989

12 x 36.5m (40 x 120ft), it has a steel-trussed roof spanning between brick load-bearing walls. Before any design work could start, the steel trusses were braced for seismic loading with diagonal steel tubing. Old and new are acknowledged with clear colour coding: the new steel has been painted light grey, while the original structure is white.

The perimeter of the shell is lined with fully or partially enclosed offices. Other work-stations are arranged in rows separated by low partitions, which are angled away from the orthogonal geometry of the building. These partitions create internal streets and the informal meeting places that are now considered so essential to the creative working process. The height of the existing building shell made possible the insertion of a mezzanine floor, where the firm's partners make presentations to potential clients in a series of pavilions.

Fernau & Hartman's lucid, functional approach is not without grand gestures. In the centre of the foyer, an imposing staircase made of concrete, steel and maple leads to the mezzanine level. Based on a slightly cranked dog-leg plan, the stair's forced perspective dramatizes the climb, while its crisp delineation of material connections serves as a potent visual metaphor for SGB's approach to graphic design. Rising from a concrete plinth, a pair of steel wide-flange girders form the stair's stringers. Treads are a composite of maple strips on plywood bolted at the edges to steel frame supports. Tension cables strung horizontally between slim steel uprights form a minimal balustrade. The stair's tough, industrial aesthetic is clearly inspired by the existing building. The steelwork supporting the stair and mezzanine is painted black, identifying a further layer of intervention.

The apparently arbitrary positions and angles of the staircase, new steel columns and beams are the result of deliberately aligning these elements with the existing structural beam and column lines on the floor below. The outcome is a dynamic, revealing mix of elements, each telling a story about what it is doing and how it was made.

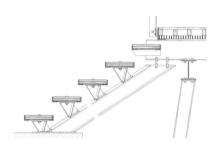

Long section through staircase

right *Inspired by the warehouse's original structure, the stair embraces a severe industrial aesthetic of steel and concrete.*

below *Treads of maple and plywood are bolted at the edges to steel frame supports. Steel tension cables form a slender balustrade.*

Nexus World Kashii in Fukuoka, Japan, forms part of a new town on land reclaimed from Hakata Bay. The developers see the new community as a link between rapidly westernizing Japan and the West and, in housing at least, as offering some interesting models for the future. They commissioned Japanese and Western architects, including Steven Holl, Christian de Portzamparc and Mark Mack, to design a series of showpiece, low-rise condominiums.

MARK MACK
KASHII CONDOMINIUM, FUKUOKA, 1992

Occupying a prominent corner location, Mark Mack's building is an exercise in joinery on several levels. The site lies at an intersection of a residential street on the east side and a more commercial street on the south side. Its position suggested two buildings, one open to the sun facing south, which would incorporate commercial space, and a less public, east-facing block. Two predominant colours have been used to reinforce the impression of the building as two distinctive elements. An intense orange-red is used in the lower building block and a strong yellow on the south elevation, which is framed by grey end walls, structural frame and top floor. The south-west corner of the lower block fits into a notch cut into the north-east corner of the higher block, a joint suggestive of cabinet-making.

This carpentry image is emphasized by the south elevation, which has duplex apartments set into the structural frame, like large drawers.

Mack's composition infuses the abstract geometry of Modernism with the richness of the work of Luis Barragán, a Mexican architect renowned for his sumptuous and radical use of colour. The blocks contain a mixture of duplexes, courtyard houses and apartments and no two units are exactly alike. Interior colours elaborate on the elevational treatments and introduce black and green on furniture, cabinets and doors.

As space is often limited, Mack ingeniously combines storage and circulation in a single element – a stepped cabinet in each apartment that doubles as a staircase. Beautifully and precisely crafted, the stepped wooden cabinet is a modern interpretation of a *tansu*, a traditional Japanese chest of drawers. The timber frame is clad in plywood panels that are stained red, yellow, black and green to create a subtle mosaic of colour. Solid and free-standing, without a balustrade or handrail, the stair/cabinet leads up to a roof terrace. Unorthodox and inventive, it epitomizes Mack's responsive approach to design.

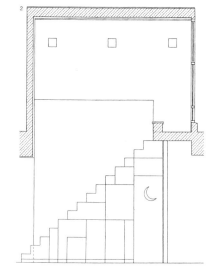

Elevation of staircase

above *Immaculately crafted from stained plywood panels, the staircase is a contemporary version of a traditional Japanese chest of drawers.*

right *Serving as both an internal staircase and usable storage space, the stair is a satisfyingly solid piece of furniture. Its subtle colours and simple geometry fuse Western and Japanese influences.*

The original Shelley House was built in 1962 during the first generation of the postwar re-planning of London Wall, an area that is currently undergoing a major regeneration and is developing as an extension of the City of London business community. Designed by Sheppard Robson, the new Shelley House is a sleek, twelve-storey office block which is equipped for the rigours of modern office life.

SHEPPARD ROBSON
SHELLEY HOUSE, LONDON, 1998

above *Springing effortlessly from floor to floor, the elegant helical staircase rises three storeys from its well at lower ground floor up to the mezzanine-balcony level at first floor.*

The building incorporates a generous double-height entrance foyer on its north-west corner addressing London Wall. This foyer is animated by a helical staircase that appears to float in space, rising three storeys from its well at lower ground floor up to the mezzanine-balcony level at first floor. The outer parts of the stair are perceived as minimal edges, giving the impression that the stair is hovering unsupported. The only obvious points of support are provided by cantilevered concrete beams clad in white-painted plasterboard at ground- and first-floor landings. The stair seems to spring effortlessly from floor to floor, reached from each landing across a glass bridge that hovers over the supporting beams. The polished plaster soffit curls upward and tapers up to the leading edge of the stair, reinforcing the sensation that the treads are floating without the structural depth of a stringer to support them.

The inner steel stringer is fabricated from rolled flat steel sheets that coil upward from lower ground to the first-floor balcony like a stretched tube to provide the main structural support. Radial treads of solid oak are supported by steel cantilever brackets welded to the inner stringer, concealed behind oak risers and the plaster soffit. The inner steel stringer extends to become the inner balustrade. Both these and the polished plaster soffit are painted a dark pewter spray finish to denote a homogeneous structural element, in contrast to the lighter wooden treads and the handrails. The handrails of both the inner and outer balustrades are made of bronze tubing, which has been left to patinate naturally with use over time. The four mid-rails of the outer balustrade are of smaller section polished stainless-steel tubes fixed to pewter-painted double-flat balusters. The lightness of the outer balustrade allows the edge of the oak treads and risers to be exposed, emphasizing the contrast between the inner and the outer parts of the stair.

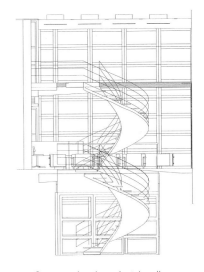

Cross section through stairwell

right *The foyer is enlivened by a helical staircase that seems to float, unsupported from above or below. The outer parts of the stair are perceived as minimal edges, furthering this appearance.*

Always interested in construction and technology, Theo Hotz is perhaps Switzerland's equivalent of a British High Tech architect. But his approach differs in some crucial ways from British practice. The protectionist Swiss habit of using only local consultants has prevented Hotz from working with British engineers. Unable to exploit inventive structural solutions as intrinsic to his architecture, he instead tends to treat structure as merely a

THEO HOTZ
CONFERENCE CENTRE, ZURICH, 1991

neutral, functional framework. Architectural interest comes from the spaces that are shaped within this framework and from the modelling of the outer envelope.

Completed in 1991, the Grünenhof Conference Centre exemplifies Hotz's meticulous, analytical approach in the context of a tight urban site in central Zurich, Switzerland. Like most European cities, Zurich's townscape is defined and shaped by blocks wrapped around a central court. Hotz was asked to design a small conference centre in the middle of an existing courtyard, which would function as an addition to the surrounding office buildings. Concealed in the courtyard, the building has no public face, yet Hotz has managed to instill it with a strong sense of drama.

Responding to the scale of the surrounding buildings, the conference centre is conceived as a three-storey box placed on top of a much smaller ground-floor podium. This arrangement of box on podium minimizes the building mass at ground level, so freeing up the courtyard as an external communal space. The ground level houses a small entrance lobby and elevators that whisk visitors aloft to the upper levels. The organization of the building is simple and legible. A conference suite and a large meeting room occupy the first floor. The second floor is entirely given over to a double-height auditorium, with a capacity of around 650. A series of enclosed bridges at ground- and second-floor levels link the conference centre to the existing buildings.

Meeting rooms and auditoria are flanked by a large foyer and break-out space overlooking the courtyard. This short end becomes the main elevation, but only by virtue of the fact that it is not pressed hard up against the existing offices as the other three sides are. Exploring a language of transparency and lightness, the entire

left *Solidity and lightness are united in one dynamically orchestrated composition as the stair sweeps through the conference centre foyer. Treads and risers made of thin steel plate evoke a crisply folded sheet of paper.*

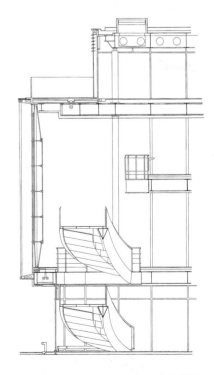

Cross section through staircase

155

above *Like a Swiss watch, the stair has an incisively engineered refinement that combines precision and elegance.*

right *At night, the spiralling steel structure becomes the focus of attention in the small internal courtyard, spectacularly displayed in its illuminated glass box.*

building is clad in a clear glass skin, so that it appears as a delicately transparent box floating above the ground. The ethereality of the external envelope contrasts with the enclosed volumes of the meeting rooms inside.

The focal element of the foyer – and indeed of the building – is a sinuously curving staircase that begins on the ground floor and rises up through the double-height foyer to the second floor. Sweeping languidly through space, the staircase inscribes a semicircle in plan. Handsomely proportioned, it resembles the grand stair in a theatre foyer. The interplay between inside and outside space and the change from the transparency of the external envelope to the mass and solidity of the walls enclosing the internal spaces is expressed through the form and materiality of the staircase: the solid supporting beam, the perforated underside of the stairs, the sheet-steel infill on the inner balustrade and the open filigree railings on the outer face. Solidity and lightness are united in one dynamically orchestrated composition.

The sweeping stair is supported by a steel structure. A curved steel beam forms the inner stringer and principal structural support. The rest of the stair effectively cantilevers off this main beam. Fin-like steel brackets 12mm (½in) thick span between the beam and the outer stringer. The depth of the stair structure decreases dramatically on its outer face, where a notched steel stringer rests on a curved steel edge beam. The entire outer assembly is only 180mm (7in) deep, compared with a 600mm (23⅝in) depth on the inside, another variation on the theme of mass and lightness.

Treads and risers are formed from folded steel plate 8mm (⁵⁄₁₆in) thick finished with a layer of black linoleum on a cork base. The steel plate projects over the outer edge of the stair, its extreme thinness and crispness like a sheet of folded paper, dematerializing the curve of the staircase. Tread nosings and risers are faced with 4mm (⁵⁄₃₂in) thick stainless-steel sheet for added durability. The underside of the stair is clad in perforated aluminium panels, painted white, which span between the fin-like stair support brackets.

Balusters are made from two white-painted steel flats topped by a tubular stainless-steel handrail. On the inner face, the balustrade is infilled by solid white-painted steel panels; on the outside, a trio of slim steel tubes form sleek horizontal railings. Thus, although the basic structure is identical, the treatment of the balustrade on the inner and outer faces further exemplifies a strong material and formal contrast.

More than sixty years since its opening, the De La Warr Pavilion in Bexhill still feels dangerously radical for the English seaside. Designed by the German Expressionist architect Erich Mendelsohn in partnership with Serge Chermayeff, it is a landmark in the history of British modern architecture. Built in 1935 as part of Bexhill's drive to boost both its residential and its tourist population, it extends languidly along the seafront like a big,

MENDELSOHN & CHERMAYEFF
DE LA WARR PAVILION, BEXHILL, 1935

right Remarkable for its fusion of sleek, nautical lines and refined detailing, the pavilion is an imposing presence on the seafront. Poised in its glass tower, the beautiful south stairwell exudes languid elegance.

below A distinctive rigid pendant light fitting hangs in the open stairwell. This has been lovingly restored. All the chrome discs and the original tubes were retained and rechromed.

white luxury liner. The decision to build a seaside entertainment pavilion was originally taken by the town council in the early 1930s and a seafront site acquired. But when the ninth Earl De La Warr was elected mayor in 1932, he persuaded the council to develop the existing site itself and took personal charge of the project. An open competition to find a design was won by Mendelsohn and Chermayeff and in December 1935, the citizens of cautious, conservative Bexhill took possession of one of the most striking Modern Movement buildings completed in Britain before World War II.

Remarkable for its fusion of sleek, nautical lines and elegant detailing, the pavilion commands the seafront, framed between sea and sky. Airily poised in a clear glass tower, one of its most striking features is its beautiful south stairwell. Influenced by the industrial staircase structures of Walter Gropius and Adolf Meyer (in particular the 1914 Werkbund Exhibition Factory in Cologne with twin spiral staircases encased in semicircular steel and glass towers), Mendelsohn and Chermayeff employed a similar means of expressing the staircase tower as a primary element at Bexhill. On the south elevation, a semicircular glass staircase tower marks a hinge point between the two wings of the building, between the theatre at one end and the restaurant and lounge spaces at the other. Inside, an open-welled spiral staircase sweeps up two storeys. The stair is placed at the turning point of the plan and celebrates the cardinal movement from floor to floor. With its centrally suspended light-fitting of neon strips and balloons accentuating the sunny steps of golden travertine and the snaking metal balustrade, it is a potent reminder of the confidence and optimism of the new inter-war architecture.

The stair structure is built of reinforced concrete, a pioneering use of a relatively new material at the time. The slenderness of structure achieved by engineer Felix

Samuely was considered very daring and innovative and a mesmerizing demonstration of concrete's potential. Uprights for the painted steel balustrade were cast into the edge of the stair structure. A gleaming, swirling aluminium handrail made from a tube attached to a T-section completes the composition. (A second inner handrail was subsequently added during the 1950s.)

Although refined, the De La Warr Pavilion is not a particularly robust building. It was not designed to withstand the battering and corrosive effect of sea, rain and storms over time and its survival highlights a number of problems relating to the preservation of Modern Movement buildings and how they can successfully be adapted to meet new demands. By the late 1980s the pavilion faced problems of serious decay as well as the difficulty of reconciling the changing dictates of the leisure and entertainment industries. To secure the funds needed to repair and regenerate the building, its perceived role had to change from that of a local amenity to a regional arts centre attracting audiences from a wide stretch of the south coast and its hinterland. In 1991 a masterplan by John McAslan & Partners (then Troughton McAslan) won a competition to restore the building while rejuvenating its public amenities. By the year 2000, three phases of renovation had been executed under McAslan's guidance, with further stages awaited. Mendelsohn's expressive and romantic architecture struck a resonant chord with McAslan and had a strong impact on the latter's own work.

Despite evidence of dilapidation and alterations elsewhere in the building, relatively little restoration work was required on the south staircase. There were some minor cracks in the terrazzo, which were repaired, and the balustrade was repainted. The distinctive rigid

above *With this centrally suspended light fitting of neon strips and balloons accentuating the steps of golden travertine and the metal balustrade, the staircase embodies the confidence and optimism of inter-war architecture.*

left *The swirling staircase provides spectacular views of the sea as its winds up to the terraces and promenade decks above. In the recent ongoing programme of restoration, the stair required relatively little remedial work to bring it back to its original splendour.*

pendant light fitting in the stairwell was also restored. All the chrome discs and, where possible, the original tubes were retained and rechromed. Slimmer fluorescent tube lamps were fitted and a concealed coupling joint fabricated within the top disc so that the light can be turned to enable replacement of the lamps. The curved external balustrades on the stair tower, which had badly corroded, were replaced with galvanized high-grade steel. McAslan's painstaking repair of the pavilion's fabric and the reinstatement of interior finishes and fittings has shown the potential for recreating the dynamic ethos of a building that has achieved an iconic status in the canon of British Modernism.

On a site near the seashore in the Japanese town of Ashiya, Chitoshi Kihara has built a memorable house that synthesizes Japanese and Western influences. The client, who had been living near the site since childhood, requested a large villa for his family with all modern conveniences as well as traditional Japanese tatami rooms (calm, austere spaces with tatami matting on the floor). Empathizing with the client's idea of living naturally,

CHITOSHI KIHARA
HOUSE, ASHIYA, 1993

left *Designed to look light and floating, the stair follows an L-shaped plan. The extreme refinement of both materials and detailing furthers this appearance of ethereality. Steel was used for the structure, but was clad in timber to ensure that the organic spirit of the house was respected.*

Kihara positioned a hall at the centre of the house to act as a fluid, permeable space in touch with the elements. The hall is enclosed on two sides by moveable screen walls made from gridded timber panels. When the screen walls are open, wind and sun penetrate and animate the double-height space, strengthening the house's relationship with nature and the elements. Sea breezes waft through the hall from south to north and sun percolates through the skylight on the ridge of its pitched roof. In the centre, a rare tree is planted. The hall represents *"ma"* space, a buffer zone between Western-style rooms and traditional Japanese domestic space. Although the Japanese way of living has changed radically and traditional architectural elements have gradually been lost, traditional domestic space is necessary for certain special events of the year, ceremonies, and other more quotidian functions.

Like his compatriot Tadao Ando, Chitoshi Kihara reinterprets the immemorial, elemental aspects of Japanese architecture such as the effects of light, minimal materiality and man's relationship with nature. As explored by architects such as Kihara and Ando, the relationship between the Western and Japanese architectural cultures has a fascinating resonance. Most Japanese now live in Western-style houses or apartments, but there is still an acute awareness of the traditions of the past. For this seaside house, Chitoshi Kihara revives traditional spaces and devices in a contemporary manner by unifying them with a modern domestic setting. As in historical Japanese architecture, he contrives an explicit connection with nature, not only in the central staircase hall, but also in the series of tatami rooms located on the ground floor. The model for this profound relationship with the natural world has its origins in Kyoto temple architecture.

The cluster of rooms overlooks an immaculately landscaped garden and pool, enclosed by lightweight *shoji* screens made from rice paper. When the *shoji* are opened, the rooms look as though they are floating against the landscape; when closed, the flickering lights of the pool cast shimmering reflections on the *shoji*. Thus two very different spatial experiences can be enjoyed by the inhabitants. Similarly, the gridded timber panels both

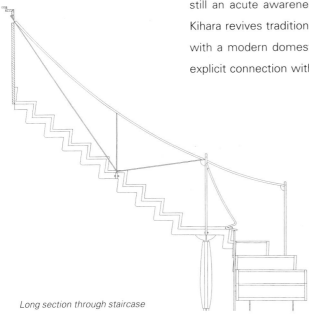

Long section through staircase

enclose and reveal the stair hall; yet even when the timber screens are closed, light filters through the grid like a gauze, casting hazy shadows around the central pivotal space.

Living accommodation is divided into two wings on either side of the hall. On the east side are the conventional living, dining and kitchen spaces. On the west, the series of tatami rooms are connected to a traditional veranda. On the upper floor, the same arrangement prevails, with a child's bedroom on the east side and tatami rooms for sleeping on the other side of the hall. The two floors are connected by a remarkable staircase that rises up through the central hall. Designed to appear light and floating, the stair follows an L-shaped plan and runs up the north side of the hall. A long straight flight of nine steps is linked by an intermediate landing to a secondary, partly curved flight of five steps. Extreme refinement of materials and detailing enhances the stair's ethereal nature. Steel was selected for the structure as it minimized the stair profile, but it is clad in timber to be more in keeping with the organic spirit of the house.

The stair structure is formed from 6mm (¼in) steel plate. Treads and risers are finished in 25mm (1in) thick sections of oak screwed to the steel to form a smooth, homogeneous surface. The underside of the stair is clad in very thin (6mm [¼in]) oak pieces. To keep the profile of the stair as slender as possible, additional support is provided by steel tensile rods made from 9 x 25mm (⅜ x 1in) flat steel members. These form a suspension structure, fixed to the head of the stair, halfway down the straight flight and the landing. Suspension points are hinged to allow for movement.

The landing is supported by a short column made of 9mm (⅜in) steel flats. The steel is clad in gently curved oak pieces that help to give the column its slightly bulbous appearance. An exquisitely minimal handrail of oak is lightly supported by a pair of 25mm (1in) diameter tubular steel uprights. As it rises up the stair, the handrail distends in a shallow curve, as if made from rope. The final flourish is a fine brass tube 21mm (⅞in) in diameter that forms the handrail for the smaller secondary flight. From the intermediate landing it spirals down to meet a steel upright. The tops of the uprights are made of 50mm (2in) deep knobs of Chinese quince. The same minimal balustrade runs around the walkway at the upper level overlooking the hall below.

Although the stair is designed to intrude as little as possible into the space, its meticulously detailed and highly unusual form gives it a compelling presence. Framed alternately by the gridded timber screen walls or by open sky, it subtly reinforces the elemental character of the house and demonstrates the consummate skill of its designer.

above *The intermediate landing is supported by a short column made of steel flats and clad in gently curved oak pieces.*

right *When the central hall is open, the staircase is poetically framed by the open sky, connecting with nature and subtly reinforcing the elemental character of the house. The thin, curved balustrade has an exquisite delicacy and fragility.*

Situated on the Franco-German border, the French city of Strasbourg contains some of Europe's most important legal and political institutions, notably the European Court of Human Rights and the European Parliament. When it became clear that the latter had outgrown its original bunker-like headquarters, an international competition was held to design a more physically appropriate building on a new site. The winning scheme by French

ARCHITECTURE STUDIO
EUROPEAN PARLIAMENT, STRASBOURG, 1999

practice Architecture Studio exudes more than a whiff of Parisian *grand projet*, being a stolid abstraction of the inherently complex notions of European political power and identity.

The new parliament building pushes up hard against the perimeter of the triangular site. As a result its plan bears an undeniable resemblance to a Napoleonic bicorne hat – in three dimensions, this evolves into a giant inclined hemicycle penetrated by a cylinder. The monumental geometry indicates the division of the building's functions into two separate yet interactive blocks. A long internal street separates the hemicycle of the main debating chamber from the cylinder housing parliamentarians' offices. Open galleries, walkways and various vertical circulation elements punctuate and animate the street as politicians, press and public scuttle around the heroically scaled space.

The most spectacular element of vertical circulation is a sweeping double-helix staircase that swirls majestically up five storeys. In a conventional double-helix form, two stairs of equal diameter spiral upward about a common centre, but begin 180 degrees apart. Architecture Studio's version is a modern variation on this theme, consisting of two helical stairs of differing lengths that connect with open galleries on each side of the internal street. One helix rises the full five storeys, while the other begins at first-floor level and rises only two storeys. The slightly abbreviated form of the staircase was doubtless dictated by practical considerations, but the effect achieved is highly dramatic nonetheless as the two stairs weave perfectly choreographed spirals through the vast space. Sinuous fluidity of form is matched by material refinement. The concrete structure, cased in white Carrare marble, is precisely honed and articulated, while a minimal, curved, clear glass balustrade topped by a handrail with a metal profile and wooden rail adds to the impression of effortless elegance.

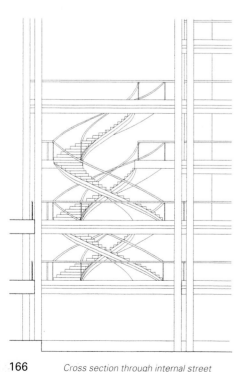

Cross section through internal street

In the Chamberi district of Madrid, just north of the city centre, there still survive a few large period villas, known locally as *palacetes*, dating from the turn of the last century. One such house was occupied by a British Council school for twenty years. When the time came to expand the Council's operations, architects Jestico & Whiles were commissioned to integrate a cultural centre, offices and exhibition space into the protected historic

JESTICO & WHILES
BRITISH COUNCIL OFFICES, MADRID, 1993

left *Forming a sympathetic modern counterpoint to the grand historic villa, a lightweight steel stair connects with the two upper floors. Perforated treads allow light to percolate down from an elliptical skylight above.*

structure. The outcome is a quietly impressive testimony to the power of the architectural imagination. The existing building has been rigorously restored, and an adjoining coach-house has been transformed into a cool, modern annexe that is linked to the main *palacete* by an elegant steel and glass footbridge.

An innovative solar control device, consisting of an oval etched-glass panel set in an inverted cone, brings natural light down from a new curved rooflight into the solid mass of the main building, while an elliptical diaphragm blind, made of fabric stretched on a metal frame, rotates on its axis to control air flow. The conversion owes much of its success to the careful articulation of vertical circulation. Inserting the dramatic top-lit cone allows light to penetrate through all three levels, illuminating the existing classical stone staircase that serves the first floor. The elliptical stairwell echoes the form of the skylight and the diaphragm blind above.

A new lightweight metal stair connects with the two upper floors, its crisp modernity forming a sympathetic counterpoint to the building's historic fabric. The new staircase's treads are made of perforated, darkened steel and are cantilevered off a central spinal steel structure. The fine perforations and gauzy transparency of the treads allow light to percolate down through the stair. Slim polished stainless-steel handrails and balusters also impart a sense of lightness and elegance. At its lower termination, the stair load is picked up at the last intermediate landing by three thin stainless-steel struts, inclined like the fingers of an outstretched hand.

Without compromising the integrity of the original building, Jestico & Whiles resolve the conjunction of the old and new stairs with skill and style. The new stair also provides an alternative means of escape, replacing an old external escape stair. Throughout the project, the architects skilfully exploit a clearly contemporary form to augment the historical qualities of the host building without any suggestion of servility. The new spiral system with its luminous rooflight is used to powerful effect, complementing the conventional design of the original staircase and creating a dramatic foil to the original interior.

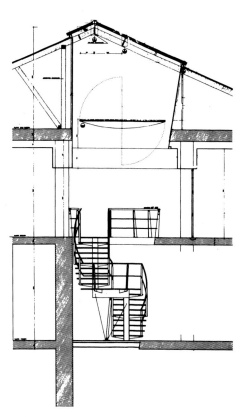

Cross section through staircase

169

Confounding the traditional and now rapidly receding conception of libraries as daunting, hermetic institutions, Alsop & Störmer's new Peckham Library in south London is bold, streetwise and iconoclastic – deliberately so. In a fragmented inner-city landscape, the building stands out as a conspicuous beacon of renewal and enlightenment. Seeking to engage with the community that it serves, and also to add vigour to the urban realm it

ALSOP & STORMER
PECKHAM LIBRARY, LONDON, 2000

inhabits, the library forms part of a major renewal programme of the area, which includes a public square, an urban gateway and a centre for healthy living.

Set on the north edge of a new public square, the six-storey building is partly clad in a reptilian skin of jade-green-patinated copper panels. On the north elevation, the copper gives way to a shimmering, kaleidoscopic wall of clear and coloured glass. Slender raked steel columns support the horizontal library volume which extends out from a narrow vertical administration block to form an inverted L-shape. Access is by means of a glazed lift that rises through the vertical block as a postcard panorama of London unfolds to the north, filtered and transformed by the coloured glass wall.

Hoisted above the blare and throb of the streets below, the luminous double-height library space resembles a quiet attic room. A trio of ovoid pods on angular concrete stilts stalk through the space. These bulbous containers variously house a children's activity area, an Afro-Caribbean literature centre and a meeting room. A spiral staircase runs up to the Afro-Caribbean literature pod from the main library volume.

Modestly scaled, to continue the theme of almost domestic intimacy, the stair is crisply yet robustly detailed. Steel outriggers radiate out from a central newel to support hardwood treads. Anti-slip discs run along the lip of each tread, like mosaics. The balustrade is formed from steel flat sections infilled with panels of finely woven stainless-steel mesh. Handrails of tubular stainless steel gently curve around the outer and inner edges of the stair, like very fine pieces of silver ribbon. On the outer edge, a second handrail was added 100mm (4in) above the lower rail. Entirely appropriate to its function, the staircase combines an unassuming dignity with a robust elegance.

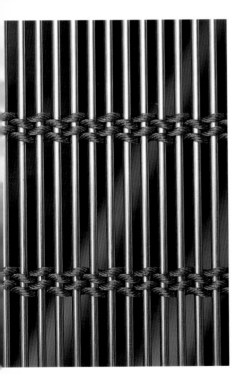

above *Detail of the woven steel mesh balustrade. Care was taken to ensure that the mesh was fine enough to prevent children's fingers from getting stuck.*

right *The modestly-scaled spiral stair links the Afro-Caribbean literature area with the main volume of the library below. Robustly detailed to withstand energetic public use, the stair structure consists of steel outriggers radiating out from a central newel to support hardwood treads. A fine mesh balustrade and tubular steel handrail complete the composition.*

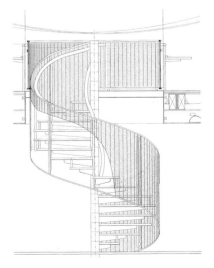

Elevation of the staircase

INDEX

Page numbers in *italics* refer to illustrations

ACKNOWLEDGMENTS

Author's Acknowledgments
Thanks are due to all the architectural practices who contributed
information and material for this book. Thanks should also go to my
colleagues on *The Architectural Review*, the staff at the RIBA Library and
my partner Malcolm Frost for collective and individual acts of support.

Photographic Credits
AKG, London: **8**, **11**; Erich Lessing **9**

Alsop and Störmer: **170 right**

Tadao Ando Architect & Associates: **70 right**; Mitsuo Matsuoka **70 left**, **71**

Arcaid/Alberto Piovano/Architect: Eric Parry Architects **65**, **66–7**; Richard
Bryant **17**; Architect: Eva Jiricna Architects Limited, **22**, **23 right**, **24 left**, **38**,
39 right, **40**, **41**; Architect: John Young **46 left**, **46–7 top**, **48**, **49**, **54–5 top**;
Architect: Eva Jiricna Architects Limited: **56–7**, **57 right**; Architect: Eric
Mendelsohn and Troughton McAslan **160–1**, **161**; Jeremy Cockayne/
Architect: Studio BAAD **116 bottom**, **117**; Joe Cornish **13 right**; Dennis
Gilbert/Architect: Rick Mather Architects **84 left**, **84–5 top**; John Edward
Linden **6–7**; Architects: Richard Rogers and Partners: **42 bottom left**, **42–3**;
Piers Paiba/Architect: Alsop & Störmer **170 left**; Paul Raferty/Architects:
Richard Rogers and Partners **44–5**

Architecture Research Office in collaboration with Guy Nordenson
and Associates: **29 top**

Arquitectonica: **135 top left**, **135 bottom left**

Architecture Studio: **166**; Gaston **167**

Axiom Photographic Agency/Chris Caldicott **10**, **15**; Jim Holmes **12–13**;
James Morris **14**; Architect: Sir Norman Foster and Partners **96**, **98**

Studio BAAD Architects: **116 top**

Bach and Mora: **69 top**

Richard Barnes/Architect: Mack Architects, Venice, California **150 left**, **151**

Barthélémy Grino Architectes SA: **113 left**; Tabou **112**, **113 right**

Architektbüro Bienefeld: **110 left**

Pierre Botschi Architects: **144 right**; Ken Kirkwood **144 left**, **145**

Brandlhuber and Kniess and Partner: **128 right**

Brookes Stacey Randall: **18–19**, **36**, **37 top**, **37 bottom**

James Carpenter Design: **20 bottom right**; Brian Gulick **20 left**, **20 top right**, **21**

Lluis Casals/Bach & Mora Architects **68**, **69 bottom**

David Churchill/Architect: Page and Park **127**

Richard Davies/Architect: Future Systems **50**, **51**, **52 left**, **53**

Diederen Dirrix van Wylick Architecten: **61**; Arthur Bagen **60**

Esto Photographics/Scott Francis/Architect: Richard Meier and Partners **62
left**, **62 top right**, **63**

Fernau and Hartman Architects: **148 top**; Richard Barnes **148 bottom**, **149**

Petra Flath/Architect: Theo Hotz ag Architekten + Planer, Zurich **154–5**, **156
left**, **156–7**

Sir Norman Foster & Partners: **78 right**, **99**

Michael Freeman/Architect: Kiyoshi Kasai **132–3**

Future Systems: **52 right**

Glasgow 99/Phil Sayer/Architect: Page and Park **126**

Nicholas Grimshaw & Partners Ltd: **34 bottom**

Guillermo Vázquez Consuegra Arquitecto: **74**, **83 left**, **91 right**; Hisao Suzuki
82, **83 right**

Gullichsen Kairamo Vormala Arkkitehdit KY: **121 left**; Simo Rista **120**,
121 right

Fritz Hack Architekt: **122 left**, **122–3**, **124**, **125**

Herzog & de Meuron: **118 left**

Steven Holl Architects: **141**

Theo Hotz Architekten + Planer, Zurich: **109 left**, **155**; Markus Fischer,
Zurich **109**, **109 right**

Japan Architect Co. Ltd/Shinkenchiku-sha/Architect: Tadao Ando Architect
& Associates **70**, **71**, **72**, **73**

Jestico + Whiles: **169**; Reto Halme **168**

Eva Jiricna Architects Limited: **23 top left**, **25 bottom**, **55 bottom**,
56 bottom

Kiyoshi Kasai architect: **132 left**

Chitoshi Kihara Architects and Associates: **163**; Yoshihara Matsumura **162**,
164, **165**

Balthazaar Korab: **16**

John Edward Linden/Architect: Richard Rogers Partnership **32**

Duccio Malagamba/Architect: Guillermo Vázquez Consuegra Arquitecto **75**,
76, **77**, **90**, **91 left**; Architect: Rafael Moneo Arquitecto **146**, **147**

Mack Architects, Venice, California: **150 right**

Rick Mather Architects: **85 bottom**

Norman McGrath/Architect: New York City Housing Authority **104**, **104–5**,
106–7 top, **107 right**; Architect: Arquitectonica **134**, **135 right**, **136 left**,
136–7; Architect: Pei Cobb Freed & Partners Architects LLP **87**

Richard Meier & Partners: **62 bottom right**

New York City Housing Authority: **106 bottom**

Page and Park: **126 right**

Eric Parry Architects: **64**; Martin Charles **66 left**

Pei Cobb Freed & Partners Architects LLP: **86 bottom**; Koji Horiuchi **89–9**;
Leonard Jacobson **86 top**, **89 right**

Alan Power Architects: **92 right**

Pringle Brandon: **100 top**; Morley Von Sternberg **100 bottom**, **101**

Purple/Ian Schrager Hotels/Architect: Philippe Starck **138 right**; Todd Eberle
138 left; Tom Vack **139**

Jo Reid and John Peck/Architect: Nicholas Grimshaw and Partners Ltd **34–5
top**, **35 top**, **35 bottom**

Christian Richters/Architect: Herzog and de Meuron **118**, **119**

Richard Rogers Partnership: **33**, **45 bottom right**, **114 left**; Architect: John
Young **47 bottom**; Katsuhisa Kida **30**; Masaaki Sekiya **31**; Paul Wakefield
114 right

Lukas Roth/Architect: Architektbüro Bienefeld **5**, **110–11 right**; Architect:
Architekturbüro Böhm **102–3**; Architect: Brandlhuber and Kniess **128 left**,
129

Sheppard Robson: **152 right**; Alan Williams **152 left**, **153**

Stratton Reekie/Roderick Coyne **171** Architect: Alsop and Störmer

View/Peter Cook/Architect: Eva Jiricna Architects Limited **25 top**, **54 right**;
Architect: Alvise Marsoni **58–9**; Architect: Richard Rogers Partnership **115**;
Architect: Eric Mendelsohn and Troughton McAslan **158**, **159**; Dennis
Gilbert **2**; Architect: Sir Norman Foster and Partners **78 left**, **79**, **80**, **81**, **97**;
Architect: Rick Mather **130–1**; Chris Gascoigne/Architect: Alan Power
Architects **92 left**, **93**, **94–5**, **95 right**

Paul Warchol Photography Inc./Architect: Architecture Research Office **26
left**, **26–7**, **28**, **29 bottom right**; Architect: Steven Holl Architects **140**,
142, **143 right**